THE DESKTOP
PHOTOGRAPHER

THE DESKTOP
PHOTOGRAPHER

HOW TO MAKE GREAT PHOTOGRAPHS WITH YOUR COMPUTER

Tim Daly

press
élan
A GENERAL PUBLISHING IMPRINT

Conceived, designed, and produced by
Quarto Publishing plc
The Old Brewery
6 Blundell Street
London N7 9BH

Project editor: Marie-Claire Muir
Art editor: Karla Jennings
Assistant art director: Penny Cobb
Designer: James Lawrence
Picture research: Sandra Assersohn
Copy editor: Ian Burley
Indexer: Diana Le Core

Art director: Moira Clinch
Publisher: Piers Spence

Manufactured by
Universal Graphics Pte Ltd., Singapore
Printed by
Star Standard Industries Pte Ltd., Singapore

CONTENTS

CAMERAS, COMPUTERS, AND SOFTWARE 8

01.1 How your computer works   10
02.1 How a digital camera works   18
03.1 How a scanner works   28
04.1 Software applications   38

PHOTOGRAPHY   50

05.1 Tips for taking better pictures   52
06.1 Improving your photographs   64
07.1 Coloring photographs   72
08.1 Mixing, merging, and montage   80
09.1 Creative effects   88
10.1 People and portraits   96
11.1 Landscapes and places   104

PRINT AND PUBLICATION   112

12.1 Printing out   114
13.1 Creative print projects   122
14.1 Preparing photos for email
      and the Internet   130

TROUBLESHOOTING AND WEBSITES   136
GLOSSARY   137
INDEX   140
CREDITS   144

INTRODUCTION

THE DAWN OF THE 21ST CENTURY HAS SEEN REMARKABLE ADVANCES IN TECHNOLOGY, AND TODAY'S DIGITAL CAMERAS OFFER UNPARALLELED EASE OF USE AND SUPERB PICTURE QUALITY AT PRICES TO SUIT MOST BUDGETS. THERE HAS NEVER BEEN A BETTER TIME TO GO DIGITAL.

If you're the sort of photographer who waits anxiously for your prints to be returned from the processing lab, then digital is definitely for you. Say goodbye to film, chemical developers, and hanging around—digital photography will change the way you shoot and create memorable images forever.

Linking seamlessly with today's powerful home computers and high quality inkjet printers, the digital camera makes producing photographs at home easy, fast, and reliable. But it goes further than that: digital images are internet ready—for emailing to friends, uploading to online processing labs, or posting directly to your website. If you enjoy the Internet community, then a digital camera offers the fastest way to share your news across the world.

This book contains all the information you need to buy and try. Impartial advice on hardware, peripherals, and the types of camera available is followed by a close look at the four most popular image editing applications. Great photographs are the result of skilled anticipation and planning, but good software can play its part too. With its facility to "reverse out" of a bad creative decision, today's software is designed with the new user in mind.

Simple explanations of essential background technology will help you avoid common pitfalls before you put your camera into action. For those new to photography, there are numerous tips on taking better photos using straightforward techniques. For those already familiar with digital cameras, there's advice on how to correct, enhance, and manipulate your way out of disappointing results, and rescue routines for unforeseen disasters like red-eye and distracting backgrounds.

More adventurous readers will appreciate projects that guide them step-by-step through a range of creative techniques, together with tricks for merging and joining images. In-depth descriptions of tools and processes common to all software applications are central to each project.

Packed with information, advice, and expert-user tips— together with valuable online resources for shareware, software, and web-based printing and editing services—this is your ideal companion in the new world of digital photography.

HOW TO USE THIS BOOK

Information is presented in module-like Units covering three broad areas—the kit (Cameras, Computers, and Software, p 8); creative techniques (Photography, p 50); and output (Print and Publication, p 112). Each chapter breaks down into accessible, topic-based headings to put the information you need at your fingertips, fast.

MENUS
Menus, palettes, and other dialog boxes are pictured and their functions explained in detail.

UNIT HEADERS
Unit 4 (Software applications), Section 5 (Adobe Photoshop). Want to know if Photoshop is the right package for you? Start here.

TOOLBOX
Screengrabs illustrate the toolbox as it would appear on your screen—no more confusion over which button to use.

THE BOTTOM LINE
Applications are assessed for ease of use (Entry-level to Professional) and cost (1 money bag for the cheapest, 5 for the most expensive).

THE BOTTOM LINE

COST:
Upgrades are usually a third of the full price.

LEVEL: Professional

TRIAL VERSIONS for download:
www.adobe.com

STEP-BY-STEP PROJECTS
Test your growing skill and creativity with guided projects.

INFORMATION
Each project is graded by difficulty level (where 1 is the most basic level and 5 the most advanced) and time taken to complete. Projects increase in complexity as the book progresses.

TIP BOX
Expert tips and tricks of the trade are revealed here!

CROSS REFERENCES
Instant redirection to other relevant units in the book.

SHORTCUT BOX
Avoid multi-menu selections with these pro keyboard shortcuts.

Unit 01: How your computer works

01.1 Internal components   10
01.2 Monitors, color, and keyboard   12
01.3 External add-ons   14
01.4 Computer platforms   16

Unit 02: How a digital camera works

02.1 What is a digital camera?   18
02.2 Types of cameras   20
02.3 Camera functions   22
02.4 Image capture quality   24
02.5 Transferring photos to your computer   26

Unit 03: How a scanner works

03.1 Flatbed scanning   28
03.2 Scanner controls   30
03.3 Scanning photographs and artwork   32
03.4 Scanning 3-D objects   34
03.5 Film scanning and scan-to-disk services   36

Unit 04: Software applications

04.1 Universal commands and tools   38
04.2 Preview and plug-in applications   40
04.3 MGI PhotoSuite   42
04.4 Adobe Photoshop Elements   44
04.5 Adobe Photoshop   46
04.6 JASC PaintShop Pro 7   48

CAMERAS
COMPUTERS
AND SOFTWARE

UNIT 01.1

HOW YOUR COMPUTER WORKS →
INTERNAL COMPONENTS

YOU DON'T NEED TO BE A WHIZ KID TO UNDERSTAND HOW A COMPUTER WORKS.

PURCHASING TIPS

Computer specifications are constantly upgraded, which means prices can drop significantly. If you have a limited budget, you'll get much more for your money if you shop online and if you hunt down last year's stock. Beforehand, it's a good idea to buy a computer magazine with a comparative listing of different brands, models, and their prices. This essential research will also help you to spot the online bargains.

Many computer resellers offer "bundles," which are discounted computer kits including printers, scanners, and software, but even though their prices are attractive, make sure that every element is suitable.

PROCESSOR

The processor works like the engine of your computer, crunching calculations at lightning speed. Like automobiles, you can buy computers with fast engines, the speed of which is described in megahertz (MHz), which really means 1 million cycles per second. The very latest models run at speeds of up to 2GHz (gigahertz; 1GHz=1000MHz), but top speed is less important than a well-set-up workstation. Some computers are fitted with two processors, which make easy work of complex image files.

RAM

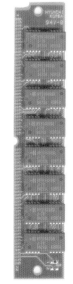

Random Access Memory (RAM), like the processor, is an internal component that does not appear on your screen. RAM is the part of your computer that stores open data when applications and documents are in use. All data held in RAM is lost when you switch your computer off or when it crashes, so it is essential to save your work to disk regularly. Because digital image files are much bigger than word-processing documents, creative workstations need much more RAM than a general-purpose computer. RAM is relatively inexpensive nowadays, so a good starting point is 128Mb (megabytes), but if your budget can stretch to 256Mb or more, you'll really notice the difference.

Once your application runs out of RAM, slower "virtual" memory takes over. Virtual memory is a clever device that treats a part of your hard drive as substitute RAM so you can keep working. Buying a computer that has vacant bays for adding extra RAM later on is a good idea.

RANDOM ACCESS
MEMORY (RAM)

PERIPHERAL
CABLING

HARD DISK OR DRIVE

A computer's hard drive or hard disk is used for storing less urgent data, like unused documents and unopened applications. Just like a library full of books, the hard drive keeps an enormous quantity of data, but you alone are responsible for organizing it properly.

Most hard drives are made in huge capacities such as 30GB (gigabytes) and have fast spin speeds. Quick-spinning disks allow faster reading and writing of data, which allows you to work at top speed. Many computers have a vacant internal space called an expansion bay, which can be used for installing a second, or even third hard drive.

A MODERN PC has outlets for additional drives and ports.

HARD DISK

OPERATING SYSTEMS

Windows, Mac OS, Linux, and Unix are all different types of system-operating software. The operating system dictates the appearance of your desktop and allows you to organize and arrange your work, but its real job is to make sure that hardware and software talk to each other—much as the human nervous system passes messages from the brain to the muscles in the body.

Operating systems are constantly developed and updated to let you have a more intuitive working experience, and also to keep up with the latest technological developments. Most external add-ons, such as scanners and printers, are designed around a specific operating system, but free updates are readily available.

PORTS

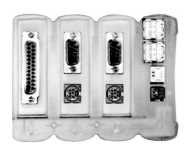

PORTS FOR CONNECTING PERIPHERALS

Used to connect your computer to an external device like a scanner or printer, ports are in fact merely special sockets. Like other components, ports have been developed over the years to allow faster transfer of large volumes of digital data. Parallel, Serial, SCSI, USB, and Firewire are all different types of connectors used by peripherals, and need to be plugged into a corresponding socket in the back of your computer. You must check that your computer has the right port before buying a new external device—and if it doesn't, don't! Instead, check out the price for an upgrade card. Other ports are used to connect the monitor, speakers, mouse, keyboard, network cable, and telephone cable for connecting to the Internet.

UNIT 01.2

HOW YOUR COMPUTER WORKS →
MONITORS, COLOR, AND KEYBOARD

YOU WOULD NEVER PAINT A PICTURE WHILE WEARING ROSE-TINTED GLASSES; IT IS EQUALLY IMPORTANT TO START YOUR CREATIVE COMPUTING WITH A CLEAN, CLEAR, AND CORRECTLY CALIBRATED DISPLAY.

APPLE iMAC

MONITORS

The human eye is capable of detecting a vast range of different colors: a computer monitor is a lot less sophisticated. Monitors are divided into two types, the bulbous cathode ray tube (CRT), and the flat-panel thin film transistor (TFT). For desktop photography, the monitor is the most important piece of your computer workstation and, like a good-quality camera lens, it lets you see sharp and color-corrected images at all times.

Like a TV set, monitors have a fixed lifespan of around five years and do not reproduce accurate colors indefinitely, so resist the temptation to skimp on a secondhand model.

DYNAMIC RANGE All images, whether printed on paper or viewed on a monitor screen, are limited by the inherent limitations of the display medium. The term "dynamic range" is often used to describe the capability of a digital device to show detail in the deepest shadows and the brightest highlights. Monitors have a much smaller dynamic range compared to photo prints or human vision. The image viewed on your monitor can never equal the printed version. Accepting this fact will prevent later disappointment.

DOES SIZE COUNT? Bigger monitor models, like the 17-inch and 19-inch, are better for creative computing because applications like Photoshop take up a lot of desktop space and leave little for your image window. If you have a

SETTING UP DIRECTIONS

WINDOWS PC:
Go to **Start > Settings > Control Panel > Display > Settings**.
Set Colors to True Color 24-bit and Screen Area to 800 x 600 or higher.

APPLE MAC:
Go to **Apple Menu > Control Panels > Monitors**.

For Color Depth, select Millions of Color and for Resolution choose either 800 x 600 or higher.

limited budget, spend your money on a computer with a mid-speed processor, if this allows you to buy a good 19-inch monitor from a reputable maker like Sony, Mitsubishi, or La Ciè.

FLAT PANELS Flat-panel monitors are the latest development and are designed to take up less desk space than CRTs. Costing about three times more than normal monitors, they need careful positioning to stop unwanted reflections.

COLOR DISPLAY You can set your monitor to display a number of different colors. It is not a good idea to view delicately colored images on a reduced color setting, so set it to a minimum of **Millions**. Lesser settings, such as 256 or even Thousands, will not let you see your image in its true colors. All monitors should be color-calibrated using software tools like Adobe Gamma, rather than the basic front-panel switches and controls.

COLOR CALIBRATION As with a television screen, you can alter the contrast, brightness, and color balance of a computer monitor, but if you want to ensure your monitor is set up to reflect the true color and brightness of your images, you'll need to calibrate it first. If your monitor is not calibrated properly, your prints will look unexpectedly different than their on-screen versions.

CALIBRATION TOOLS All computers are supplied with color calibration software tools that help you to set up your workstation correctly. A popular tool found on both Windows PC and Macintosh platforms is the Adobe Gamma color calibration application. If you are not sure where this is located, do a Start>Find>Files or Folders (PC) or Sherlock (Mac) command. Once opened, Adobe Gamma is very easy to operate, prompting you to make alterations where necessary. On completion, these neutral color balance settings are saved and referred to each time you switch your computer on and off.

FLAT-PANEL MONITOR

SCREEN RESOLUTION

All computers allow you to alter the resolution of your monitor so you can set a comfortable working display. Screen resolutions are measured in pixels and are known as 640 x 480 (VGA), 800 x 600 (SVGA), 1024 x 768 (XGA), and above. Very high-resolution settings make type and tools quite small and fairly difficult to see, so a mid-range setting will serve you better.

MOUSE AND KEYBOARD

Both of these are input devices allowing you to dictate your work in progress. Although drawing with a mouse is not straightforward at first, plenty of practice will make you an expert

KEYBOARD AND MOUSE

UNIT 01.3

HOW YOUR COMPUTER WORKS →
EXTERNAL ADD-ONS

PERIPHERALS ALLOW YOU TO CAPTURE AND TRANSFER IMAGES FOR PRINTING AND LONG-TERM STORAGE.

FLATBED SCANNER

Even the most basic flatbed scanner will capture more information than you really need to make quality prints from your desktop computer. With the significant drop in scanner prices, all workstations should be equipped with one. Better models are those made by manufacturers who also make professional scanning equipment, such as Umax, Canon, Epson, and Heidelberg. Optional or bundled transparency hoods for budget scanners very rarely deliver value for money, and often give disappointing results.

FLATBED SCANNER

FILM SCANNER

INTERNET CONNECTION

Although most modern computers connect to the Internet through an internal modem, older models need to use an external device. Access to the Internet is vital if you want to attach digital photos to your emails, create your own web site, and download special software updates, shareware, and plug-ins.

FILM SCANNER

For desktop photographers, a better bet is a dedicated film scanner. A different kind of device designed to capture data from tiny negative and transparency films, a budget film scanner is about four times the cost of an entry-level flatbed. With this kind of peripheral you can shoot conventional film with a normal camera, then scan to make digital prints. A mid-price 35mm scanner can pull out enough detail from a 35mm original to make a 16½ x 11¾ -inch photo-quality print.

You can get much better results scanning film than from prints, especially poor-quality photo-store-processed enprints. If you have hundreds of unprinted negatives or slides in a bottom drawer, a film scanner allows you to bring them to life.

PRINTER

Like scanners, inkjet printers have dropped in price, and a top-quality model can be bought for less than $300. Printers are graded by the type of ink cartridge they use, such as three, four, or six colors. For best-quality photo prints, go for a six-ink model. Most printers can use special-size and -shape papers like panoramic and postcards.

All printers are connected to your computer through either a USB, Parallel, or Serial port, so if you have an older computer, check to see that it has the corresponding socket before you buy a new one. A recent innovation is the card-slot printer, which accepts a digital camera memory card and prints without the need for a computer.

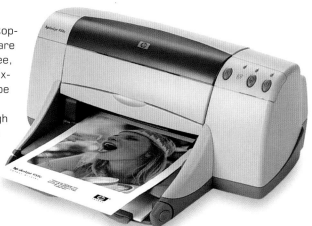

INKJET PRINTER

DIGITAL CAMERA CARD READER

The card reader, which resembles a small disk drive, greatly speeds up the transfer of data from a digital camera memory card. Better ones use USB or Firewire connections, but the others, like the floppy disk flashpath adapter, are painfully slow.

DIGITAL CAMERA
CARD READER

REMOVABLE MEDIA

If you want to transport images to another computer or send images off for specialist printing, CD writers, available as either internal or external models, are available. CD-R disks can hold a massive 650Mb of data and, at less then $1.50 each, are by far the cheapest way to store and transport your images safely. Floppy disks are all but useless for digital photography (although there is a limited range of cameras based on floppy disk storage). A Zip drive, using 100Mb or 250Mb rewritable disks, is a well-recognized format, however, at eight times the cost of CD-R disks, Zip disks are expensive.

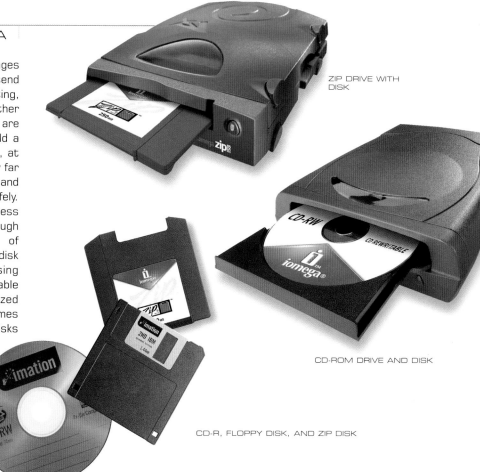

ZIP DRIVE WITH
DISK

CD-ROM DRIVE AND DISK

CD-R, FLOPPY DISK, AND ZIP DISK

UNIT 01.4

HOW YOUR COMPUTER WORKS →
COMPUTER PLATFORMS

THERE'S NO NEED TO WORRY ABOUT PICKING THE WRONG TYPE OF COMPUTER: BOTH POPULAR PLATFORMS ARE ON SPEAKING TERMS THESE DAYS. YOUR DECISION TO PURCHASE SHOULD REST ON YOUR OWN PERSONAL TASTE.

APPLE MAC OR WINDOWS PC?

There are two dominant computer platforms to choose between—Apple (Mac) and the generic Microsoft Windows. (Computers running Windows are commonly referred to as PCs, although technically this means nothing more than personal computer.) So how do you decide which one is right for you? Apple computers are traditionally used by designers in the creative industries, while PCs are found in every office and business in the world. Apple has recently been at the cutting edge of computer design as well as technical innovation for running data-intensive applications like Photoshop and video-editing software. Both are used in schools and universities across the world. It's not an easy choice to make.

APPLE MAC

WINDOWS PC

While Windows PCs tend to be cheaper, the price difference between Apple and Windows-based machines is negligible, so your decision really lies on personal preference and willingness to get involved in the technicalities when things go wrong. All Apple computers are designed and built with standard internal parts, which forces third-party companies responsible for making printers and scanners to comply with a rigid set of standards. There is less likelihood of new things not working unless you are sold the wrong part by mistake.

Windows PCs, despite being made by lots of different companies worldwide from a grab bag of non-standard internal parts, are also subject to common standards. Here again, there is little difference between the platforms.

If you are new to digital photography and want to keep all the complicated, technical stuff very much in the background and get on with the enjoyable activity, then an Apple Mac may be the best choice.

Don't be duped by marketing speak claiming speeds of this or that many times that of the competition. The performances of top-spec machines of both varieties are broadly similar despite their different engines. Perhaps only in graphic-intense applications, such as image- or movie-editing software, does the Mac platform have a slight edge.

SWAPPING FILES BETWEEN TWO PLATFORMS You may have heard that it is impossible to swap disks and files between the two platforms. This is simply not true. If you have a PC at work and a Mac at home, it is very easy to read the same files on both systems, providing you insert a file extension at the end of your document name and use PC-formatted media.

The golden rule for swapping files between the two platforms is to make sure your removable media—CD-R, Zip, or floppy—is PC-formatted. Apple computers can read and write to both Mac and PC-formatted media, but PCs can only use PC-formatted disks.

FILE EXTENSIONS For Apple users, the next rule to ensure cross-platform compatibility is to make sure your files are always saved with the three or four letter/number file extension. Used at the end of a file name like "landscape.tif," the extension allows an application to recognize one of its permissible formats. If the file has no extension, it will not open on a PC.

UNIT 02.1

HOW A DIGITAL CAMERA WORKS →
WHAT IS A DIGITAL CAMERA?

WITH SO MANY MODELS TO CHOOSE FROM, BUYING A DIGITAL CAMERA CAN SEEM PERILOUS, BUT WITH MODERN CAMERA SPECIFICATIONS NOW WELL BEYOND THE BASIC, EVEN A BUDGET MODEL WILL GIVE YOU GREAT RESULTS.

FLASH
SHUTTER RELEASE
VIEWFINDER
LENS COVER
LENS
BATTERY/MEMORY CARD

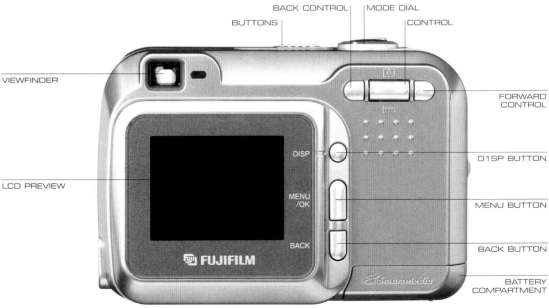

BACK CONTROL
BUTTONS
MODE DIAL
CONTROL
VIEWFINDER
FORWARD CONTROL
DISP
D1SP BUTTON
LCD PREVIEW
MENU /OK
MENU BUTTON
BACK
BACK BUTTON
BATTERY COMPARTMENT

PIXELS

Digital cameras are fitted with a light-sensitive patch called a "charged coupled device" (CCD). Under a microscope the CCD looks like a honeycomb, with each cell acting like a mini light receptor. The cells are subjected to light via the camera lens and become filled with light rays. The degree to which they are filled corresponds with how bright a pixel (short for "picture element") becomes. Each cell makes a pixel, and better cameras are fitted with sensors that produce an image with more than a million pixels. The more pixels, the larger you can make a print.

BATTERY CHARGER AND POWER ADAPTOR

POWER SUPPLY

Because digital cameras do not need to house bulky film canisters, mechanical winders, and mirrors, they can be made smaller and lighter than their non-digital counterparts. However, because they rely totally on electrical power to operate, they are entirely and hungrily dependent on batteries. Only buy a digital camera if it has rechargeable batteries and an AC adapter included in the basic kit.

LIQUID CRYSTAL DISPLAY (LCD)

Unlike conventional cameras, digitals have an extra gadget for composing the photograph—the rear LCD preview screen. At a couple of inches in size and showing a live real-time playback (like a video camera), the LCD allows you time to check your photo without squinting through a tiny viewfinder. Even more impressive, you can use the LCD for playing back and previewing images. Chopped-off heads, a thumb over the lens, and portraits with the subject blinking are now things of the past.

CARD READER

STORAGE Once captured, images are transferred immediately to the camera's memory card, where they can be stored, displayed, and previewed, or even erased. Memory cards are available in many different capacities, like video cassettes, allowing you to store more images should you be unable to return to your computer.

PREVIEW After returning home from your shoot, the images can be previewed on a normal TV by using the camera's Video Out cable. To transfer to your computer, use a camera-to-computer cable, or remove the camera memory card and insert it into a special card reader. Once the images are transferred, you can safely erase the memory card, making it ready to use again and again.

MAKING MOVIES Many cameras can capture desktop movies and sound.

Small and low-quality images are repeatedly taken, up to 15 per second, then sequenced together like a video. These are suitable for desktop rather than television playback.

The latest cameras are designed to take advantage of the convergence of all kinds of consumer technology, and can be plugged directly into printers and commercial printing services, although without the opportunity of creative intervention. Some cameras can even be attached to a mobile phone for wireless transmission of images as email attachments.

SMARTMEDIA AND COMPACTFLASH CARDS

UNIT 02.3

HOW A DIGITAL CAMERA WORKS →
CAMERA FUNCTIONS

WITH AN ARRAY OF SWITCHES, DIALS, AND MENU BUTTONS, IT CAN BE A CHALLENGE JUST TO SWITCH A DIGITAL CAMERA ON AND OFF. THE ALL-IMPORTANT FUNCTIONS ARE EXPLAINED HERE.

Instead of the mechanical shutter used in a film camera, digital compacts use an electronic shutter, so you do not hear the familiar "clunk" when you take a picture. For newcomers to digital photography, the absence of this familiar noise can make it tricky to know whether you have taken a picture or not.

TAKING PHOTOS

INTERNATIONAL STANDARDS ORGANISATION (ISO) SPEEDS Like the speed of traditional film, the sensors used in digital cameras are made to work best at lowest ISO speeds, such as 100 or 200. Better cameras can be set to work within a range such as 100–800 ISO, but, like faster films, high-speed settings produce a speckled effect called "noise." This unwanted by-product appears in shadow areas of photographs, looking like bright red or green pixels.

200 ISO

800 ISO

FLASH All digital compacts have built-in flash units that can vary in strength. On a budget camera, a flash is really only effective for lighting a small room, or for fill-flash photographs. Most are not powerful enough to light up subjects more than 5 yards away, producing dark and disappointing results. Only SLRs and the superior compacts have connecting sockets to attach a better flashgun.

LCD MONITOR All cameras have a rear LCD preview screen, used for real-time framing and to check whether your photograph has been successful. The LCD is also used to display menus, settings, and edit controls, but it can drain battery power quickly!

THE LCD PREVIEW lets you scroll through your shots for editing.

RELYING ON THE LCD PREVIEW

It is impossible to tell from the tiny LCD screen whether your image is in perfect focus, and this can sometimes give a false sense of security. If in any doubt, take another frame, or use your camera's Video Out port to preview on a TV.

EDITING

IN-CAMERA It is not vital to buy the largest-capacity memory card, as you can delete unwanted photographs individually in-camera. All cameras let you delete single images or groups in folders, or wipe the entire card for immediate reshooting. Unlike conventional film, there is no need to print or even keep your mistakes.

VIDEO OUT SOCKET If you do not want to edit your work on location, you can connect your camera to a TV and edit your pictures before transferring them to your computer. You may be surprised at the quality once your images appear on screen, and, best of all, the event can be shared with family and friends.

SOUND AND VIDEO RECORDING Many compacts allow you to make short desktop-quality movies, limited in length only by the size of your memory card. These are usually saved in the MPEG format, which can be played back on any computer. On the very latest cameras, verbal sound clips can also be recorded for each still image.

DESKTOP VIDEO CLIPS can be played back on a variety of players such as Windows Media Player or Quicktime. Players work like traditional video recorders, allowing you to fast forward, pause, and rewind your video clip.

WHITE BALANCE

If you have ever had orange- or green-colored photo prints after shooting in artificial light, you will be pleased to learn that digital cameras have a white balance function to correct these problems. If you want to shoot photos where domestic lightbulbs or fluorescent tubes are the sole source of light, use your white balance setting to compensate. Remember to switch it back when shooting outside.

SHOT UNDER DOMESTIC TUNGSTEN LIGHTING, the photo on the left was taken with the white balance set on Daylight. To correct this, switch the Tungsten Balance setting on.

SHOT UNDER DOMESTIC FLUORESCENT LIGHTING, the photo on the left was taken with the white balance set to daylight, resulting in a characteristic green color cast. To correct this, try using the Fluorescent Tube setting. Better cameras have different white balance settings for each common type of tube, like warm white or cool white.

HOW A DIGITAL CAMERA WORKS →
TRANSFERRING PHOTOS
TO YOUR COMPUTER

SETTING YOUR COMPUTER UP PROPERLY IN THE FIRST PLACE IS THE MOST DEMANDING PART OF TRANSFERRING DIGITAL IMAGES. IF YOU DO ENCOUNTER PROBLEMS, HERE ARE A FEW COMMON REMEDIES TO TRY.

HANDLING MEMORY CARDS

SmartMedia cards should be handled very carefully after being removed from the camera, without touching the gold contact. CompactFlash cards are thicker and more rugged, but care should be taken to ensure that the two rows of tiny sockets on the bottom edge are not damaged or obstructed by dust or grit. Never handle cards near sand or water, and always put them back in the camera when finished.

SMARTMEDIA MEMORY CARDS

GETTING DRIVER SOFTWARE UPDATES

If you are using new gadgets like digital cameras or card readers on older computers, there can sometimes be a problem with compatibility. The easiest way to solve this problem is to visit the peripheral manufacturer's web site where you will find free driver updates for instant download. Once downloaded, follow the installation instructions.

COMPACT DIGITAL WITH A LARGE CAPACITY MEMORY CARD

DOWNLOADING

Once you have captured and stored images on your camera memory card, the next step is to transfer them to your computer. In the process of downloading image files from your camera, identical copies of your files are created and stored on your computer, leaving originals untouched and still on the memory card.

DIRECTLY FROM THE CAMERA Before this can happen, you must load the camera driver software onto your computer. If you have never installed software before, all you need to do is to follow the prompts and step-by-step instructions after inserting the disk. Wait until installation is complete, then Restart your computer.

Before using the software, create a shortcut icon to sit on your desktop so that all you have to do is an easy double mouse click to start it running. Connect the camera and plug it into the mains via its AC adaptor. Open the software and click on Acquire or Download, and watch your images appear as thumbnails. To download each image fully, click on the thumbnail of your choice and wait for the larger image to appear. Use the File>Save command immediately and, to keep it at its best, save it in the TIFF file format. The image can now be opened in your creative application.

CARD READER

TROUBLESHOOTING CHECKLIST

IF THE MEMORY CARD ICON DOES NOT APPEAR ON THE DESKTOP, check the following:
- Have you inserted the card in the reader the right way?
- Have you plugged the reader into the right computer port?
- If all else fails, restart your computer with the card reader cable removed.

USING A DIGITAL WALLET Instead of carrying extra memory cards or a heavy laptop on location, a recent innovation is the pocket-size portable hard drive. Memory cards are docked into the device and downloaded, and are ready to be used again in-camera. The latest drives offer enormous capacities in the range of 10–20Gb, and are ideal if you plan to spend months away from home.

MICRODRIVE MEMORY CARD WITH ADAPTOR FOR DOWNLOAD

FROM A CARD READER

Install the card reader software and restart the computer. Insert the memory card into the reader and then connect it to the computer through the right port. Your card will then appear on your desktop just like a floppy disk or CD icon. Double click it, then drag and drop the files into a folder on your hard drive. Once transferred, your image files are ready for you to open and manipulate. Do not double click the tiny image icons to open them, as this often launches a basic application called an image viewer. As the name suggests, a viewer only allows you to look at your images, not to change anything. A better option is to open your imaging application first and then use File>Open. Search for the image folder and hit OK. After you have opened them for the first time, make sure you save your images in the TIFF file format.

TROUBLESHOOTING CHECKLIST

IF IMAGES DO NOT DOWNLOAD, check the following:
- Is the connecting cable in the correct computer port?
- Is the camera switched on?
- Is the camera set to playback or transfer mode?
- Is the memory card empty?
- If all else fails, try restarting your computer with the camera cable in place, and try again.

UNIT 03.1

HOW A SCANNER WORKS

FLATBED SCANNING

A FLATBED SCANNER IS AN ESSENTIAL PART OF YOUR DESKTOP KIT FOR DIGITIZING ARTWORK AND PHOTOS. IT LOOKS LIKE A TINY PHOTOCOPIER, AND WORKS BY TRANSLATING REFLECTED LIGHT INTO PIXEL IMAGES.

There are three different types of scanner to consider: flatbed, film, or combination. Just like digital cameras, scanners use light detectors called CCDs, but instead of a grid-like patch, scanner sensors are made in thin strips. Set close to the sensor is a tiny light source that illuminates the subject during the scan. In operation, each tiny sensor cell is responsible for making a single pixel in the digital image.

SCANNER RESOLUTION

Put simply, resolution is just another term for quality. The more tiny sensors your scanner has, the more detail it can capture from your original photograph. The more pixels you create, the more detail and size you can obtain in your prints. When purchasing a scanner, good quality is indicated by a resolution such as 600 dots or pixels per inch (dpi). Some flatbed scanners can capture 2400 dpi, but create more data than you really need. In terms of value for money, flatbed scanners generate far more image data than the most expensive professional digital camera, and are the cheapest and most sensible option for newcomers to digital photography.

PORTS

Like other peripherals, scanners are plugged in to your computer using either a USB, SCSI, Parallel, or Firewire port. This type of connection also indicates the speed at which data is transferred: Parallel is the slowest, SCSI and USB faster, and Firewire is well at the front.

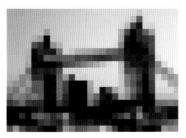

SCANNED AT 30 DPI

60 DPI

120 DPI

240 DPI

OPTICAL AND INTERPOLATION

Just to complicate the issue, many manufacturers boost the attractiveness of their scanning products by describing resolution using two different terms: optical and interpolated. The truth about resolution is given by the optical value, which describes the true hardware design of the sensor. Interpolation is just another term for enlargement, and describes how much your image can be blown up using software trickery.

The interpolation process is simple: new pixels are invented using colors based on the immediate neighborhood, which are then wedged between original pixels. Because of the high number of invented pixels, interpolated scans are never as sharp as optical scans. Even if your scanner claims to work at 9600 dpi, it will not necessarily give you good results at that setting.

THIS IMAGE WAS scanned at its highest optical setting of 600 dpi.

THE SAME IMAGE was scanned at an interpolated 3600 dpi to create more enlargement, but detail is not as sharp as expected.

COLOR DEPTH

Scanners are also graded by the number of different colors they can detect. Like an artist's color palette with a set number of paint colors, these limitations are referred to as color depth or bit depth. All recent scanners can sense a range of at least 16 million colors, sometimes referred to as a 24-bit palette. For color detection, many scanners use a super-high 42-bit palette that draws on literally billions of different colors. However, because most software and inkjet printers can only work with a 24-bit palette, this is far more than you really need. You are very unlikely to see any difference between a print made from a 42-bit scan and a 24-bit scan.

FLATBED SCANNER

FLATBED SCANNER SPECS

LOOK FOR:
Minimum Resolution: 600 dpi
Color depth: 24 bit or greater

UNIT 03.2

HOW A SCANNER WORKS →
SCANNER CONTROLS

JUST LIKE A CAMERA, A SCANNER CAN CAPTURE IMAGES IN BLACK AND WHITE OR COLOR AND HAS SIMPLE CONTROLS FOR FRAMING, CHANGING EXPOSURE, AND FINE FOCUSING.

USING A SCANNER

Scanners can be controlled in two ways—by the stand-alone scanning application, or through a software plug-in. Stand-alone software is a basic application that operates your scanner and nothing else, so your images need to be saved then reopened in your favorite imaging program if you want to work on them.

TYPICAL SCANNER SOFTWARE
INTERFACE

Plug-in software lets you control the scanner from within your favorite application and shuts off automatically once a scan is complete, leaving you free to work on your image immediately. If your scanner is a push-button type, you can launch the scanning application by pressing the button on the front of the unit.

Most scanner software has a Photoshop plug-in or is TWAIN compliant. TWAIN stands for Toolkit Without An Interesting Name, and is no more than a kind of software travel plug adapter, used to connect third-party devices like scanners and digital cameras to Adobe Photoshop and other applications.

THE MARQUEE TOOL

The marquee looks like a permanently moving rectangle and is used to frame and crop your scan image. Drag the moving lines tightly around the edges of your images to give a more accurate result and stop your file from being bigger than necessary.

CAPTURE OR INPUT RESOLUTION

There is no need to use a calculator to work this setting out, or to capture at maximum resolution just to make sure. Set this to 200 dpi if you want to make your own inkjet prints, and 72 dpi if you want to make files to email or place on your web site.

CAPTURE MODES Like shooting with different types of photographic film, capture modes determine the image mode your scan will be created in. RGB (red, green, blue) is a universal mode used for all color originals—photographs, paintings, pages from a magazine, or anything else. For monochrome originals such as black-and-white photos and pencil drawings, use the Grayscale mode. Finally, if your original is pure black and white, like text or a line diagram, use the Bitmap mode.

SCANNED IN RGB MODE

GRAYSCALE MODE

BITMAP MODE

ENLARGEMENT FACTOR This is identical to the enlarge and reduce button on a photocopier. If it is at 100%, your image will print the same size as your original. If you want to enlarge tiny originals, remember that like a photocopy, they will lose sharpness as they increase in size. Scan the biggest original you can get your hands on.

PRESET TOOLS Various auto-adjust controls can be used to make "exposure" judgements on your original image, but you may want to experiment with these to find the one that makes the least visible change. Common problems with presets are an increase in contrast, losing subtle grays and detail on the way, and unexpected color changes. If the result looks worse than the original, start over again. Your aim should be to lose little or no fine detail.

BRIGHTNESS AND CONTRAST SLIDERS If you have a low-contrast or faded image, you can set new highlights and shadows before scanning. You will get more precise control if you leave this adjustment until the image is opened in your image application.

THIS IMAGE WAS scanned without using any auto adjusters.

OCR SOFTWARE Some scanners are bundled with an OCR (Optical Character Recognition) application that can be used for converting typescript into editable word-processing documents.

FILE SIZE This tells you how much data your scan will create. Avoid using 42-bit settings, or your files will become very slow to process. The number of pixels in your image has a direct bearing on its file size, so it is very important to avoid capture overkill. Even a slight increase in capture resolution from 200–300 dpi will double your file size.

SCANNED AGAIN using an Auto Contrast command, notice the color change and increased contrast in the image.

THIS 42-BIT IMAGE has a file size of 12Mb.

REDUCED TO 24 BIT, the file size drops to 6Mb.

HOW A SCANNER WORKS →

SCANNING 3-D OBJECTS

YOU CAN SCAN THREE-DIMENSIONAL OBJECTS WITH A FLATBED SCANNER, COLLECTING IMAGES FOR LATER USE IN A MONTAGE PROJECT.

If you want to make a quick digital image of an object, scanning is a much faster way than taking a photograph. All flatbeds can see and scan one facet of an object, and they generally do a good job of it. The process is very simple and is made even easier if you can temporarily remove the scanner lid. Most models allow you to do this, primarily so that large and unwieldy books can be accommodated on the bed.

PREPARING THE SCANNER

The scanner glass bed will stay in top condition if you wipe off fingerprints with a lens cleaning cloth. To stop the glass from scratching on contact with an object, cover it with a sheet of the highest-quality clear acetate you can find. This can easily be removed when scanning prints at a later time.

CHOOSE THE SAME controls you would use for scanning a color print.

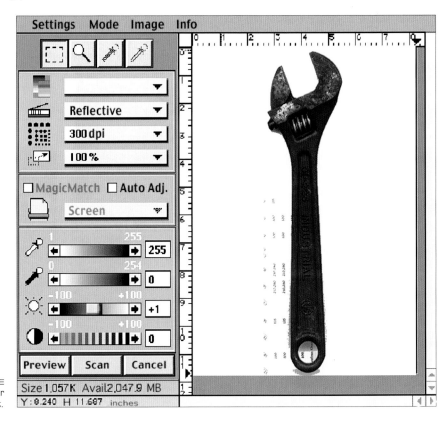

The sensor can "see" about 2 inches of sharpness from a 3-D object, but only if you mask off stray room light, which can have an adverse effect on the "exposure." Place the desired object face down, then drape a large piece of white paper over the object, covering the glass completely.

SCANNER SETTINGS
Capture mode: RGB color.
Input Resolution: 200 dpi for inkjet, 72 dpi for web output.
Filters: Sharpening OFF.
Save As: TIFF format.

MARQUEE TOOL Make sure you drag the marquee tool tightly around the object, cropping out as much of the scanner lid as you can. This makes a dramatic improvement in the quality of color and contrast.

AFTER PROCESSING

A bit more processing is required to make scans of three-dimensional objects look their best. Once scanned and saved, make sure you stick to the following sequence of commands:

1. Zoom in close and make a precise selection around your object.
2. Cut out the background.
3. Make contrast corrections to your object using Levels (see pages 80–81).
4. Try to restore an accurate color balance.

TRANSPARENT BACKGROUNDS

In order to transfer your newly cut objects to other image files, it is a good idea to leave the background behind. With better software, you can compose your image in layers, having irregular image elements floating above backgrounds or other layers. If you cannot cut away your background layer, try and change its color to something that has a contrast with your object; this will make later selection much easier.

TELLTALE SIGNS

When a scanner cannot make an accurate color match to your object, it may make bright pink or bright green pixels in error. With shiny surfaces you will spot these mistakes in the scan highlight areas, but these are easily corrected by using the Red-eye Reduction tool or a Desaturate command.

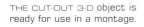
THE CUT-OUT 3-D object is ready for use in a montage.

COMBINED WITH A convincing backdrop, you'd never guess the object had been pasted in.

UNIT 04.1

SOFTWARE APPLICATIONS →
UNIVERSAL COMMANDS AND TOOLS

THERE IS A VARIETY OF COMPLEX SOFTWARE AVAILABLE, BUT MOST OF THEM SHARE COMMON TOOLS AND COMMANDS.

There is very little point in buying the most complex software package to begin with, so bundled software is well worth considering. Many digital cameras and scanners are sold with free or bundled software, like Adobe PhotoDeluxe, Adobe Photoshop Elements, or MGI Photosuite. Despite being available free or at a low cost, all of these packages share common tools and commands with the current top-of-the-range package, Adobe Photoshop 6.0.

THE RECTANGULAR MARQUEE tool makes geometric selections by dragging your cursor over the image.

SELECTING

Unlike the simple process of highlighting a word in a word-processing application in order to change its size and font, selecting a part of a digital image is more complex. There are many ways to pick up or select an area in your image so that you can change its color and tone without affecting the surroundings.

Easy tools to use are the dotted Marquees, used by dragging and stretching to fit regular geometric areas. For complex shapes, the freeform Pen or Lasso can be used to hand draw a line around the perimeter. Both of these methods fence off an area of pixels for later manipulation. The Magic Wand tool works in a very different manner. Like a magnet, the lasso here attracts pixels of similar color values, and groups them into a selection area. This is a good method to use when it's necessary to select a complex, but similar-colored area, like a blue sky in a landscape photograph.

THE MAGIC WAND selects similarly colored pixels.

CUTTING AND MASKING

If you want to replace large areas of your photographs, use cutting or erasing tools. Remember that if you cut out large areas, you need to replace them with other convincing detail. The Eraser is an easy tool to use, especially if you are tidying up the edges of a recently introduced copy-and-paste layer.

YOU CAN EITHER cut your image away, or erase the background behind it.

LAYERS

Better applications allow you to assemble your images in layers. Like a deck of playing cards, layers allow you to stack different images, artwork, and text together. The uppermost layer in the Layer palette blocks out all underlying layers, but you can alter the transparency of a layer and use different blending modes to merge the images together.

COPYING, PASTING, AND THE CLIPBOARD

If you want to take a part of one photo and blend it with another, you need to copy the area first. After selecting the area in question, an Edit>Copy command sends an identical version to your computer's clipboard. The clipboard is your computer's invisible storage area, which can contain only one packet of data at a time. The clipboard can be accessed by all applications and is a convenient way to transfer images and other files between unrelated applications. Once copied, an Edit>Paste command brings a file or image back into your chosen destination document.

A LANDSCAPE with plenty of space

…leaves room to paste in images.

PAINTING AND CLONING

All photo-manipulation applications have tools for painting and drawing, so many in fact that it is hardly worth using a separate painting or drawing program. With a variety of brush shapes and sizes, colors can be picked from a palette of millions.

Cloning is an exciting way to retouch blemishes or unnecessary details in your images by using existing pixels to paint over unwanted ones.

AN OBJECT in the background merges into the subject's head.

THE RUBBER STAMP can be used to remove it.

FILTERS

Filters work by applying creative patterns, textures, and color effects to your work. Better filters have extra controls for judging the amount of change required.

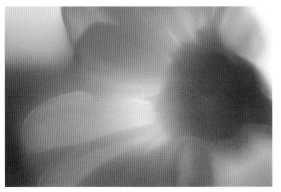

THE ORIGINAL IMAGE

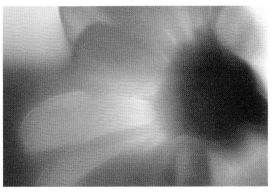

WITH A TEXTURE FILTER APPLIED

UNIT 04.3

SOFTWARE APPLICATIONS →
MGI PHOTOSUITE

WITH MANY MILLIONS OF COPIES SOLD, PHOTOSUITE IS ONE OF THE LEADING
ENTRY-LEVEL PACKAGES FOR DIGITAL PHOTOGRAPHY AND WEB GRAPHICS.

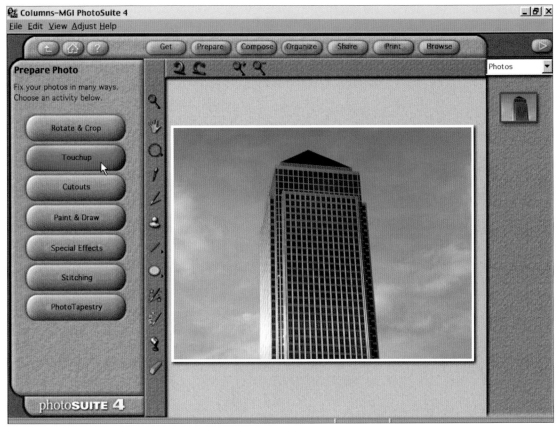

DESKTOP WORK AREA

THE BOTTOM LINE

COST: Occasionally bundled
with cameras and scanners

LEVEL: Entry level

TRIAL VERSIONS for download:
www.mgisoft.com
www.photosuite.com

With an on-screen look that sets it apart from other image-
editing software, MGI PhotoSuite presents you with simple
buttons and controls, like touch-screen shopping. It is unlike other
menu-driven applications, and beginners who are new to using
computers may find the look of this package unthreatening and a
good place to start.

TOOLS

PhotoSuite offers more than software tools for manipulation. With
extra functions for organizing, storing, and keyword searching for
your images, it helps you keep a close eye on the location of your

image files. The most frequently sought tools for repairing red-eye and restoring faded and cracked images are placed close to hand.

WEB TOOLS If you want to create your own web pages without learning HTML, PhotoSuite's instant web page creation and publishing tools let you use and adapt a huge variety of templates with your own images, text, animations, and links to other web sites.

ANIMATIONS If you want to join single images into a slide show or make them into fast-moving web graphics, PhotoSuite comes with a basic Graphics Interchange Format (GIF) editor and a function for grouping images into slide-show albums for attaching to emails.

PANORAMA STITCHING The most recent version of the software allows users to join up to 48 different digital images together to form a wrap-around panorama. This can be saved for later use in a web page as a fully navigational 360-degree view. Great for recording historic or limited access interiors, this kind of image gives you a kind of virtual-reality experience on the web.

COMPATIBILITY Made for Windows PC only. Windows 95, 98, ME, NT 4.0, 2000. Internet Explorer, essential for all web-based projects, is included.

SYSTEM REQUIREMENTS
The minimum specifications required to run this application are:
Pentium II processor, 32Mb RAM, SVGA video card, 800 x 600 display, 200Mb of free hard disk space.

KEYWORD SEARCH

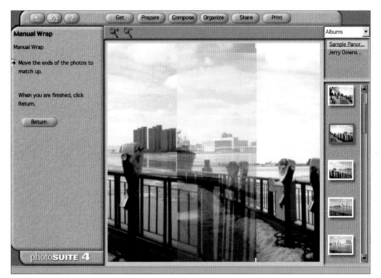
PANORAMA STITCHING FUNCTION

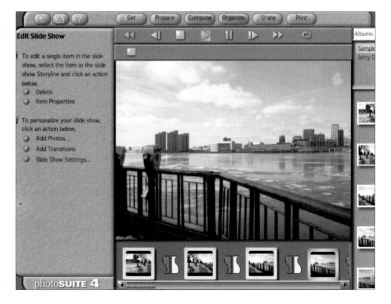
SLIDE SHOW OPTION

UNIT 04.5

SOFTWARE APPLICATIONS →
ADOBE PHOTOSHOP

ADOBE PHOTOSHOP IS THE MOST SOPHISTICATED APPLICATION FOR CREATIVE MANIPULATION THAT MONEY CAN BUY.

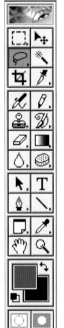

TOOLBOX

If you are planning a career in the design, publishing, or multimedia industries, Adobe Photoshop is the industry standard tool, working across both Mac and PC platforms. Able to read and save all major file formats and image modes, Photoshop is the essential software for a budding creative professional. For the digital photographer, Photoshop is a complete collection of all the camera gadgets, film effects, and darkroom secrets ever invented—and all in one place. The only drawback for a new user is how to translate the often unfamiliar terminology used by the application to describe traditional photography techniques and processes.

DESKTOP WORK AREA

THE BOTTOM LINE

COST:
Upgrades are usually a third of the full price.

LEVEL: Professional

TRIAL VERSIONS for download:
www.adobe.com

TOOLS

Designed for a wide range of professionals from wildly different backgrounds like printers, graphic designers, and photographers, Photoshop has many different tools for doing exactly the same task. Most useful of all is the innovative History Palette, which can be configured to undo up to 100 previous commands, preventing an inexperienced move from turning into a catastrophe.

Images can also be created in layers, to keep elements of your work both separate and protected from each other. As your skill and expertise develop, Photoshop presents you with more complex tools for fine-tuning image color, tone, and sharpness. If you plan to repeat your creative manipulations on later works, you can save or record any color, filter, or toning recipes used.

Despite the complexity of the program, there are many straightforward tools for toning, photomontage, and filtering. The most precise and hardest to use tools include the pen tool for making razor-sharp cut-outs, Curves controls for pushing and pulling contrast in the smallest areas, and the Duotone mode for introducing delicate-toned effects over your images.

PLUG-INS There are lots of plug-ins that can be added to Photoshop to build up a customized application, and there are hundreds of online Photoshop user resource sites, sharing tips, techniques, and home-made color recipes.

WEB TOOLS Photoshop has a useful Web Photo Gallery command which creates an instant web site from a folder of your digital images.

COMPATIBILITY Available for Mac OS 8.5, 8.6, 9.0, and X, and Windows 98, 2000, and NT.

SYSTEM REQUIREMENTS Pentium processor (Windows PC), PowerPC processor (Mac), 64Mb RAM, 125Mb free hard disk space, 800 x 600 display, CD-ROM drive.

PHOTOSHOP'S SOPHISTICATED TOOLS make complex layered projects easier.

UNIT 04.6

SOFTWARE APPLICATIONS →

JASC PAINTSHOP PRO 7

PAINTSHOP PRO 7 IS A WINDOWS PC-ONLY PACKAGE THAT PACKS IN A HUGE RANGE OF FUNCTIONS, HELPING AN INTERMEDIATE USER CREATE PROFESSIONAL RESULTS.

DESKTOP WORK AREA

THE BOTTOM LINE

COST:

LEVEL Entry level to intermediate

TRIAL VERSIONS for download
www.jasc.com

Despite being designed for the budget end of the market, PaintShop Pro shares many common tools with professional Photoshop, such as Layers, contrast-correcting Levels and the multiple-undo function Command History. In its seventh version, the package is well-conceived and benefits from a long design history.

TOOLS

Shipped without the extras of MGI PhotoSuite, PaintShop Pro is aimed primarily at the intermediate-level digital photographer. It is equipped with all the tools needed for drawing, painting, and correcting simple shooting mistakes like red-eye and scratches, plus a huge amount of sophisticated toning and coloring tools.

PaintShop Pro is an excellent package to start with, and there is enough in the package to keep you busy for a long time. With value-added features for creating animations, logos, and your own web pages, Paint Shop Pro is easy to pick up and does not place baffling technical barriers in your way.

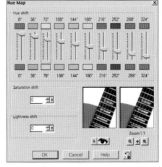

HUE MAP DIALOG

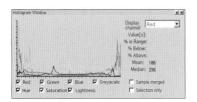

HISTOGRAM DIALOG

COLOR DIALOG

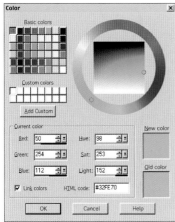

RED-EYE REMOVAL

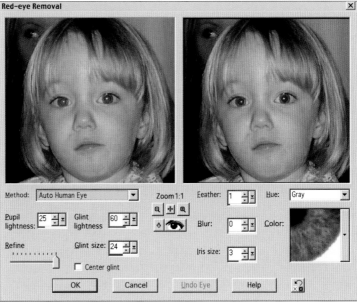

PHOTO TOOLS All popular problems, such as dust and scratches, red-eye, low contrast, and noise are catered for, plus fine-tuning tools for adjusting color saturation, color balance, and contrast. PaintShop Pro 7 can open and read nearly 50 different file formats, including Photoshop's own .psd file format, and for this reason alone, it is a worthwhile addition to a creative workstation.

WEB TOOLS For those interested in creating images for the web, PaintShop Pro has both simple and sophisticated tools for creating animations, image maps, image slicing, rollovers, and data compression.

COMPATIBILITY Available for Windows 95, 98, 2000, and NT 4.0.

SYSTEM REQUIREMENTS 500MHz speed processor, 128Mb RAM, 1024 x 768 display.

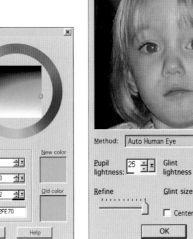

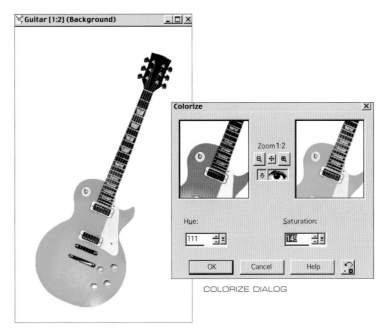

COLORIZE DIALOG

Unit 05: **Tips for taking better pictures**

05.1 Essential techniques   52
05.2 Shutter speed and aperture   54
05.3 Lens effects   56
05.4 Viewpoint and composition   58
05.5 Flash   60
05.6 Common photo problems   62

Unit 06: **Improving your photographs**

06.1 Tools   64
06.2 Cropping and resizing   66
06.3 Color and contrast   68
06.4 Sharpening up   70

Unit 07: **Coloring your photographs**

07.1 Tools   72
07.2 Global color change and sepia   74
07.3 Hand coloring with brushes   76
07.4 Multiple coloring with commands and selections   78

Unit 08: **Mixing, merging, and montage**

08.1 Tools   80
08.2 Text effects   82
08.3 Textured and translucent overlays   84
08.4 Multiple layered landscape   86

Unit 09: **Creative effects**

09.1 Filters   88
09.2 Making a watercolor painting   90
09.3 Psychedelic color, sharpness, and brightness   92
09.4 3-D rendering and warping   94

Unit 10: **People and portraits**

10.1 Selections   96
10.2 Tone effects   98
10.3 Coloring effects   100
10.4 Vignettes and diffused focus   102

Unit 11: **Landscapes and places**

11.1 Tools   104
11.2 Turning day into night   106
11.3 Making backgrounds more interesting   108
11.4 Reflections and water   110

PHOTOGRAPHY

UNIT 05.1

TIPS FOR TAKING BETTER PICTURES →
ESSENTIAL TECHNIQUES

BEFORE YOU TINKER WITH YOUR IMAGES ON THE COMPUTER, TRY TO CAPTURE YOUR SUBJECTS USING THE BEST POSSIBLE TECHNIQUES. PREPARATION, RATHER THAN EXPENSIVE EQUIPMENT, IS THE KEY TO GETTING GREAT RESULTS.

ANTICIPATION

The world's best photographers continue to produce great pictures because they have developed a knack for anticipating photo opportunities. To avoid missing a great photo, have your camera switched on, flash ready, and your index finger held over the shutter release. You can carry your camera comfortably by your side like this until the moment presents itself and when it does, all you need to do is compose and press the shutter.

HOLDING YOUR CAMERA

Blurry images and fingers accidentally draped over the lens easily occur if you don't hold your camera properly. Digital cameras can be small and awkward to use and it can be tricky to navigate menus and functions, but it does get easier with practice. The ideal way to hold your camera is to first make a clenched fist, then slide the camera inside your grip. Feel around for the camera's ergonomically placed finger and thumb holds. You don't need to keep your fingers tightly or painfully locked around the body, but if you move them around they may stray over the lens.

All digital compacts force you to compose your picture through either the LCD monitor or a separate viewfinder window, but only the LCD gives you the view through the actual lens. Once you are holding the camera, the next step is to place the palm of one hand and fingers of the other directly under the camera body. To prevent camera shake, pull your elbows in close to your body to stop the camera swaying.

LIGHT AND QUALITY

SOFT QUALITY DAYLIGHT

FULL OVERHEAD SUNSHINE

The one completely uncontrollable variable in all types of photography is natural light. All photographs look better if they were shot during soft quality daylight. This is the best lighting for accurate colors and for pin-sharp detail. Bad weather and overcast conditions make for poor color reproduction and a loss of sharpness. Full overhead sun-shine causes blacked-out shadows and burned-out highlights called "excessive contrast." Photographs of the same subject can look very different according to the kind of light they were shot under.

LIGHT DIRECTION

Always keep the light behind you when taking photographs. This means you might have to reposition yourself and your subject to ensure that you are not facing into direct sunlight. If too much direct sunlight streams into your lens you will get lens flare, which looks like a white explosion. No amount of software trickery will rescue an image with flare.

FLARE is caused by shooting into the sun

BETTER RESULTS are achieved by shooting with your back to the light

CAMERA CARE

It's very easy to improve the quality of your photographs just by giving your camera a spring clean. Over time, and with frequent use, camera lenses get marked by greasy fingers and attract static dust. Dirty lenses have a profound effect on image quality, resulting in low-contrast and weak color results. Dust and hair are responsible for making tiny light-blocking barriers that cause minute soft-focus areas on your images. As a golden rule, keep the lens cap on when the camera is not in use, and remove marks only with moist lens cleaning wipes, as they won't harm the delicate coating of your lens.

CLEAN LENSES make a better job of reproducing saturated colours

SMEARED OR GREASY lenses make low contrast and flat photography

UNIT 05.2

TIPS FOR TAKING BETTER PICTURES →
SHUTTER SPEED AND APERTURE

THE PERFECT EXPOSURE IS THE CORRECT COMBINATION OF TWO CAMERA CONTROLS: SHUTTER SPEED AND APERTURE. YET IT IS POSSIBLE TO MANIPULATE BOTH FOR PURELY CREATIVE REASONS.

All digital cameras have additional functions called program modes. These are preset controls for shooting in specific situations such as Close-up, Nighttime, Sports, Portrait, and Backlight. The program mode for each of these circumstances sets an appropriate combination of shutter speed and aperture for you so that you can carry on shooting without distraction.

COMMON CAMERA AUTO FUNCTIONS

Most digital cameras have two basic program modes: aperture priority and shutter speed priority. Aperture priority allows you to select a creative aperture setting, then the camera sets the necessary shutter speed to make a balanced exposure. Shutter speed priority is the reverse, letting you set a deliberately fast or slow speed to freeze or blur your subjects while the camera sorts out the aperture setting. For more experienced photographers, a camera with fully manual controls offers more predictable and exact results.

APERTURE

The aperture is a circular opening of a variable size, located inside the lens of your camera. The aperture controls the quantity of light passing through to the CCD sensor, much like funnels of varying diameters. Apertures are measured in "f" numbers on a standard scale: f2.8, f4, f5.6, f8, f11, f16.

The f16 end of the scale creates small apertures, or tiny holes, used to create a deep depth of field. The f2.8 end of the scale uses larger apertures, or bigger holes, to create shallow depth of field. Each step along the scale halves or doubles the amount of light exactly.

SHUTTER SPEEDS

Most digital cameras are fitted with a mechanical shutter that looks like a thin black curtain. This opens and closes at varying speeds to let light reach the sensor. Different shutter speeds can be used to create two opposite effects. Slow shutter speeds such as 1/15 second or longer will make moving objects record as a blur. Faster shutter speeds such as 1/125 second will arrest most

A SLOW SHUTTER SPEED such as 1/2 second suggests movement

DEPTH OF FIELD

"Depth of field" is a term that is used to describe the extent of sharp focus between the nearest and furthest elements in your photograph. You control depth of field by selecting the aperture that matches your creative intention. Portrait images shot with a shallow depth of field simulate closeness to the subject in real life, but landscape images shot with great depth of field allow us to see every tiny element in a scene.

USING A LARGE APERTURE, here f4, means that only the subject's eye is sharply focused

A SMALL APERTURE, here f16, gives a great sweep of sharpness from foreground to background

human motion. Very fast shutter speeds such as 1/1000 second will even freeze fast-moving subjects—a race car, for example. Shutter speeds are measured in fractions of a second along a universal scale: 1, 1/2, 1/4, 1/8, 1/15, 1/30, 1/60, 1/125, 1/250, 1/500 to 1/1000 second. These speeds double or halve exactly as you move up or down the scale.

FAST SHUTTER SPEEDS such as 1/125 second give a freeze frame effect

THE SHUTTER was on a B setting and left open for a couple of minutes

UNIT 05.3

TIPS FOR TAKING BETTER PICTURES →
LENS EFFECTS

IN ADDITION TO GETTING YOUR SUBJECTS IN SHARP FOCUS, LENSES CAN PROVIDE A WIDE RANGE OF CREATIVE EFFECTS.

FOCUS

A TELEPHOTO LENS will bring subjects closer

A WIDE-ANGLE LENS will push subjects away from you

A MACRO LENS lets you shoot at very close distances

All lenses have a set minimum focusing distance that prevents you from getting sharp results closer than a certain distance. If you are unsure about the minimum distance your camera can focus on, never get nearer than one meter from your subject. If you want to get close, stand well back and zoom in, rather than use a wide-angle close-up.

FIXED FOCAL LENGTH Digital cameras are fitted with either a fixed focal length lens or a zoom lens. If your camera has a fixed focal length lens, you need to physically move back from your subject to fit more of it in, or closer to it to fill the frame. Fine for general purpose holiday and family snaps, this kind of lens is found on cheaper camera models.

ZOOM A zoom lens is three lenses in one: wide angle, standard, and telephoto. At its wide-angle setting a zoom lens will include more of your scene in the viewfinder, "pushing" the scene away from you. It is especially useful indoors or in cramped spaces.

A FIXED FOCAL LENGTH LENS is usually a general purpose semi-wide angle

SHOOTING FOR PANORAMIC STITCHING

If you are intending to shoot a set of images to stitch together into a revolving panorama, avoid using super-wide-angle settings. When stitched together, it may be impossible to join the distorted lines seamlessly, and the illusion will be ruined. Use your lens on its mid-range or telephoto setting for best results.

At its mid-range setting, a zoom will give you a similar view to the human eye, which is fine for most outdoor subjects. At its most extended, sometimes called the "telephoto" setting, a zoom lens "pulls" far away subjects closer, so you don't have to move closer yourself. This is particularly useful for wildlife and architecture. Macro settings on zoom lenses allow you to focus on small subjects at very close range.

POINTS OF FOCUS Most digital camera lenses focus automatically. To avoid the camera locking onto the wrong focus point, you should direct the camera to focus on your subject. If you are shooting a portrait, focus on the nearest eye, not the tip of the nose, or the part of the subject closest to you.

SELECTIVE FOCUS

SELECTIVE FOCUS Combined with an aperture setting like f4 to give a shallow depth of field, you can create very subtle focusing effects. By including objects in the foreground and picking a further element to focus on, you can make a creative blur effect often used in advertising photography.

SELECTIVE FOCUS COMBINED WITH A SMALL APERTURE

DISTORTION

At both ends of the scale, lenses can create curious distortions.

WIDE-ANGLE DISTORTION Extreme wide-angle lenses, sometimes referred to as "fish-eye" lenses, make circular images that warp straight, horizontal, and vertical lines. Wide angles can be unflattering when shooting portraits close-up, as facial features will be more exaggerated and distorted. Because wide angles create unusual perspective effects, tall buildings shot from ground level will look as though they end in a sharp point.

WIDE-ANGLE DISTORTION

TELEPHOTO DISTORTION At the telephoto end of the scale, zoom lenses foreshorten or compress the physical distances in a scene. With an absence of warped lines and angles, a telephoto is best used for picking out details in far-off places, but there is little sense of how close objects are to each other.

TELEPHOTO DISTORTION

UNIT 05.4

TIPS FOR TAKING BETTER PICTURES →
VIEWPOINT AND COMPOSITION

EVEN THE MOST EXPENSIVE CAMERA WON'T GUARANTEE AWARD-WINNING RESULTS EVERY TIME. ULTIMATELY, GREAT PHOTOGRAPHS ARE MADE BY YOUR VISUAL ABILITY TO SENSE A POTENTIAL WINNER.

VIEWPOINT

Adults see the world from a similar five-foot-six kind of viewpoint, but that doesn't mean we should all take our photographs from the same position. A child's-eye view can be simulated by kneeling down to a lower level and will make the normal world appear radically

A BIRD'S-EYE VIEW

A WORM'S-EYE VIEW

different. Tall buildings will appear to tower over you, and adults will look like giants. A worm's-eye view can be created by lying on your front with your camera placed on the ground, and is a great way to exaggerate dramatic clouds in a natural landscape. If you can get a high vantage point from a bridge or tall building, you can make all your subjects appear tiny and insignificant. The position you adopt before taking a photograph is called the viewpoint, and this strongly influences shapes, perspective, and composition.

USING LINES

We live in a regular world of straight, horizontal, and vertical lines. Look out for lines and other elements that connect foreground to mid-ground to background. This dictates a kind of visual pathway for your viewer that holds their attention and draws them toward your central subject.

Diagonal lines and features can contribute to some of the most attractive photographs. You can easily transform a mundane subject into a fabulous image, just by tilting and skewing your camera. Look for straight lines and then use your own body position to place them in the opposite corners of your viewfinder.

Diagonals are also a great way to symbolize movement or activity, especially if one side of the photograph has been tilted to look "heavier" than the other. This is a kind of visual trick to make you think things are on a downhill slope.

LINES can draw attention into your photograph

SYMMETRY AND ASYMMETRY

Great composition is all about arranging picture elements in the viewfinder in a harmonious and balanced way. Simple rules make for very effective results. Perfect symmetry, where the image can be divided into two or more identical partitions has been used by painters for centuries. Composition is more about what you decide to leave outside the viewfinder.

ASYMMETRICAL COMPOSITION

SYMMETRICAL COMPOSITION

SHOOTING AROUND YOUR SUBJECT

If you are learning how to make better pictures, don't be afraid to shoot several different versions of the same image, as there's no extra expense involved with digital photography. If you can't decide where to position your subject in the frame, shoot a wide-angle version and crop it down later on your computer.

ADDING INTEREST

Just because your camera makes rectangular images, there's no reason why you can't crop them into squares or even stretch panoramics. Unusual image shapes are a great way to attract attention.

Great photographs needn't be dependent on beautiful or sumptuous surroundings. Just the two simple elements of light and shadow are enough ingredients for a fascinating observation.

PANORAMIC IMAGE SHAPE.

DIAGONAL LINES add drama to your work

STRIKING LIGHT AND SHADOW

UNIT 05.5

TIPS FOR TAKING BETTER PICTURES →
FLASH

FLASH ALLOWS YOU TO TAKE GOOD PHOTOGRAPHS IN LESS THAN PERFECT SITUATIONS, BUT IT CAN PROVE A HANDFUL IF YOU DON'T KNOW HOW IT WORKS.

FLASH BENEFITS

Apart from use in darkened situations, flash is a great tool to bring out colors. In any situation, indoors and out, flash will allow nearby objects to be reproduced with more saturated colors and show off finer detail. With its rapid burst of light—over and out in less than 1/1000 second—flash will also freeze nearby movement.

BUILT-IN AND EXTERNAL FLASH UNITS

Most digital cameras have a built-in flash unit, but they don't all have the same power. No built-in flash will be able to illuminate a subject more than 16 feet away. To light whole rooms or subjects further away, you will need to connect a more powerful flash to the hot shoe adapter of your camera (if it has one). A built-in flash cannot illuminate scenes or landscapes, only people-sized objects.

Better digital compacts are already fitted with a hot shoe for attaching external flash guns. If you are thinking of adding one to your camera kit, buy a flash from the same manufacturer as your camera, as they will be designed to work together in all modes and programs. Third party guns may still work, but they will not be dedicated to all of your camera's features.

FLASH lightens shadows and freezes movement

FLASH STRENGTHS

The strength of a flash gun is indicated by its Guide Number. This is a measurement of the furthest distance (in meters) that the flash will illuminate multiplied by the current aperture, for a particular ISO speed. For example, a flash with a guide number of 40 (100 ISO) will illuminate an object 82 feet (10m) away if your lens is set to f4 (10 x 4=40). Powerful flash units have bigger guide numbers.

SITUATIONS WHEN FLASH IS ADVISABLE

INDOORS
- When your camera won't fire because of low light
- When shooting with a bright window in the background
- When you don't want your image to take on an orange or green color cast from artificial indoor lighting

OUTDOORS
- At night
- During the daytime when there are harsh shadows cast over a portrait

FILL FLASH

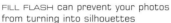

CATCH LIGHTS in a subject's eyes

FILL FLASH can prevent your photos from turning into silhouettes

For those situations when the subject would be silhouetted by an extremely bright light behind it, fill flash can be used to place much needed light into shadow areas. Great for limiting the unflattering effects of deep shadows of subject's eye sockets in portraits, the weaker fill flash complements existing daylight rather than replacing it. High contrast light is most likely during sunny days or on sunny overseas holidays. Especially useful for putting a "catch light," or the tiny white dot of light in a portraits eyes, fill flash helps avoid a lifeless result.

AVOIDING FLASH MISTAKES

Flash is a useful tool for taking pictures in poor light, but knowing its limitations will avoid later disappointment. The flash unit actually controls itself, a bit like a thermostat switching itself off when it reaches the set temperature. After the initial burst, flash light reflects back off the first object it strikes, then shuts itself off. Because of the split-second speed of this process, you are never aware of it happening. Flash photography fails when there's a closer object between you and your subject that interrupts the pathway of light. Regardless of size, any obstruction will stop your flash from hitting the right subject properly.

FLASH ERROR caused by light hitting a near object

CREATIVE TIPS

FLASH FILTERS
- If used indiscriminately, flash may produce results lacking in atmosphere. Even with built-in flash units, you can modify the light effects by making simple DIY filters. To make harsh black shadow lines softer, place a small piece of translucent paper over the unit using clear adhesive tape. Good for taking nearby portrait pictures, this diffuser will slightly reduce your flash power, but give softer, more flattering, results.

- Light from flash is always colorless or slightly on the blue side, but filters can easily change that. DIY filters are easily made with lightly colored cellophane or candy wrappers. Oranges, reds, and purples will soak your subject (particularly white or light-colored subjects) in colored light.

UNIT 05.6

TIPS FOR TAKING BETTER PICTURES →
COMMON PHOTO PROBLEMS

FEW CAMERA MANUALS TELL YOU HOW TO AVOID PROBLEMS, LET ALONE HOW TO CORRECT MISTAKES. HERE'S A SELECTION OF COMMON ERRORS AND HOW TO SOLVE THEM.

RED EYE

Red eye is often a problem if you use a built-in flash to take portraits, but it is easy to avoid. During low-light conditions, the aperture-like iris in the eye opens wide to let more light in. Red eye occurs when flash bounces back off the red surface of the inner eye, called the retina. You can avoid red eye in one of three ways:

- Use the red-eye reduction mode of your camera if it has one. This usually employs a technique that fires a low-power pre-flash to shrink your subject's iris before the main flash fires.
- Place yourself at an angle to your subject and ask the subject to avoid looking directly at the camera.
- Place your subject near a bright light source, like a table lamp, to prevent the irises in the subject's eyes from widening.

RED EYE

AUTOFOCUS ERRORS

AUTOFOCUS ERROR

Autofocus lenses don't rely on your eagle eyes to make pin-sharp pictures. Instead, the camera uses the center of the viewfinder to detect a contrasting edge between adjoining shapes in the subject. Once found, this will set the point of focus automatically. This works perfectly well for subjects placed centrally in the viewfinder, but problems occur when the center of the frame is positioned between or beyond the main subject, as the focus will be set on an object closer or further away.

Most digital cameras allow you to prefocus on a non-central subject first by depressing the shutter release halfway before recomposing and shooting.

Autofocus requires good-contrast subjects; it cannot respond to blank walls and low-contrast scenes. If your lens "hunts" or struggles repeatedly in and out of focus, prefocus on the edge of an object that is the same distance away. Unfortunately, most digital cameras have tiny LCD viewers that flatter a badly focused image.

EXPOSURE PROBLEMS EXPLAINED

TOO LIGHT OR OVEREXPOSED

CORRECTLY EXPOSED

TOO DARK OR UNDEREXPOSED

PROBLEMS SOFTWARE CAN'T SOLVE

VERY DARK OR UNDEREXPOSED IMAGES
Even if you can rescue detail using your Levels sliders, the resulting image will
be very noisy.

VERY LIGHT OR OVEREXPOSED IMAGES
Unlike photographic film, a digital image doesn't have any hidden detail lurking in highlight areas.

VERY BLOCKY OR COMPRESSED IMAGES
If your images have been compressed as low-quality JPEGs. there's no way back other than reshooting.

Inside a camera is a device for measuring the quantity of light, called a light meter. This responds to the brightest object in your viewfinder, regardless of its position, color, or size. Light meter systems are designed to avoid exposure inaccuracies caused by dominant light sources. However, none are completely foolproof. Overexposure occurs when too much light reaches the camera's image sensor, resulting in over-bright and washed-out images. Underexposure happens when too little light reaches the sensor, resulting in dark and muddy images.

Low-quality results occur when you forget that the camera doesn't know what the main emphasis or subject is. Even a tiny lightbulb occupying a fraction of the composition can influence your camera's light meter. To solve this problem, either recompose your photograph to exclude the element, or use flash.

When shooting on location, the same problem occurs, albeit on a larger scale. Outside, the sky is usually much brighter than the land, causing any ground-based elements to be recorded darker than desired. If in doubt, recompose to exclude the bright areas, take a meter reading off the ground, then recompose and shoot.

DOMINANT WHITES make other colors appear darker

AFTER RECOMPOSING and taking a meter reading from the ground, the result is much better

IMPROVING YOUR PHOTOGRAPHS →
TOOLS

THE MAIN POINT OF MANIPULATING PHOTOGRAPHS IS TO IMPROVE THEM, BUT THERE ARE A FEW SIMPLE TOOLS THAT WILL HELP CORRECT SOME OF THE MOST COMMON MISTAKES MADE DURING PHOTOGRAPHY.

CROP TOOL

The Crop tool is used to reframe your photographs. Most cameras, both digital and conventional, capture a bit more around the picture perimeter than you originally intend. With the exception of a few expensive models, a camera's viewfinder doesn't show a precise image edge and is generally designed to show a bit less rather than too much. It is disappointing when you open an image on your computer and discover unintended elements in the composition.

When shooting with a digital camera, there's little point in composing an image tightly in the viewfinder or packing the frame with edge-to-edge precision. A much better approach is to pull back slightly from the scene, either using your zoom on a slightly wide-angle setting or physically retreating from the subject. The Crop tool then lets you recompose your image by providing four new movable edges that you can drag into position. After redrawing the boundaries, everything lying outside is discarded. You can use the tool just to remove the unexpected or to make creative changes to your image shape.

UNCROPPED THE IMAGE LACKS EMPHASIS

A TIGHTER AND BETTER CROP

Cropping and resizing >
go to pages 66–67

RUBBER STAMP

Often photographs are ruined by an unexpected element. Light reflected on lens, red eye, skin blemishes, and unwanted background details can all create distractions and ruin your shot. The Rubber Stamp tool (called the Cloning Brush tool in Paint Shop Pro) can be used to copy and paste pixels from other areas of your image over the offending blemishes. In other words, instead of painting over unwanted detail with solid colors, which can look artificial, the Rubber Stamp tool uses existing image detail to make blemishes vanish and gives a very convincing result.

UNWANTED ELEMENTS can easily be removed . . .

. . . using the rubber stamp

CONTRAST TOOLS

The term "contrast" describes the relative amounts of strong blacks and whites in your image. Low-contrast images are made entirely from different shades of gray with no full blacks or whites present. High-contrast images are the opposite; they have few gray tones, but strong blacks and whites. You can manipulate contrast with lots of different tools such as Levels, Brightness, and Contrast sliders and the more complex Curves commands. Although you can also control contrast in your printer software dialog, it's much better to do it in your image-editing application first.

Color and contrast >
go to pages 68–69

LOW CONTRAST

CONTRAST RESTORED

SHARPENING FILTERS

Sharpening up > go to pages 70–71

At their most extreme, out-of-focus images have no defined shape edges and lack strong colors. Focus could, therefore, be described as a loss of contrast at the edges of individual shapes within the image. All applications have tools that can miraculously correct this bad problem. Sharpening filters restore sharp focus by increasing the contrast between each adjoining pixel. The most refined sharpening tool is the Unsharp Mask Filter (USM), which has three adjusters for precision.

UNSHARPENED

AFTER SHARPENING

UNIT 06.2

IMPROVING YOUR PHOTOGRAPHS →
CROPPING AND RESIZING

ONE OF THE WORLD'S GREATEST PHOTOGRAPHERS, HENRI CARTIER BRESSON, PRIDES HIMSELF ON HIS ABILITY TO PREVISUALIZE THE EXACT RESULT AT THE MOMENT HE PRESSES THE SHUTTER. THE REST OF US HAVE TO CROP.

CROPPING

TIGHT CROPPING by the use of a telephoto lens

Photographs allow you to communicate messages, ideas, and feelings to other people. Good photographs are those that have a direct and unambiguous approach, and leave the viewer in no doubt as to the photographer's intentions. As a photographer it's your job to emphasize and draw attention to the main elements in the image using tools such as focus, depth of field, and composition.

TO FIT DIMENSIONS If the result of a crop needs to conform to a particular shape or fixed dimension, you can preset the crop tool to do this for you. Type in the target size of your final crop and watch the tool adjust to fit. New crops can also be created in an identical height vs. length ratio by simply holding the Shift key down and dragging any of the crop box corners.

FOR BETTER COMPOSITION Used to restore symmetry or remove blank and distracting space, cropping can be an effective tool for improving your images. Sometimes it can be difficult to decide whether to take a portrait or landscape format shot, especially if the subject you're shooting doesn't immediately suggest a natural choice. Software cropping can easily convert one to the other. If you are forced to shoot from a distance, cropping can remove excessive foreground detail.

SOME LANDSCAPE FORMAT PHOTOS looks better when cropped to portrait format

ALTERING PIXEL DIMENSIONS

Cropping discards pixels to leave you with a smaller image, both in pixel dimensions and data size. It is possible to then enlarge the image, which is a bit like using the zoom function on a photocopier to produce bigger, but not necessarily sharper, images. Overly enlarged images will print out with poor levels of sharpness, but slight enlargements will exhibit hardly any noticeable degradation.

AN UNCROPPED IMAGE loses sharpness if cropped and overenlarged

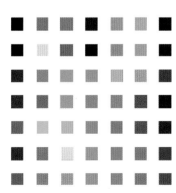

TO ENLARGE If you've cut away a chunk of your image, it will print out at a smaller size. If you do a major crop and remove a substantial area of original pixels, you may need to put some pixels back in order to make a decent sized print out. New pixels are added by a process called "resampling," in which extra pixels are slotted between existing ones. To enlarge it so you can make a bigger print, select **Image>Image Size** and make sure both Resample and Constrain Proportion check boxes are ticked (bottom left). Next, in the Document Size section, type in the size you want your image to be.

TO REDUCE Most digital cameras let you shoot photographs in a range of different pixel dimensions such as 1800 x 1200 (higher resolution) and 640 x 480 (lower resolution). If you've shot high-resolution images and want to use them on your web page, you'll need to reduce them first, or they'll be too big to be seen without scrolling. This process is the opposite of enlarging but uses exactly the same tools. In your **Image>Image Size** dialog box, make sure both Resample and Constrain Proportion are checked, then reduce the Width and Height of the Pixel Dimensions. This process effectively discards pixels across the whole image, but without cropping.

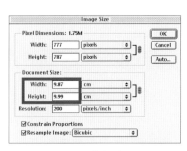

THE IMAGE SIZE dialog box

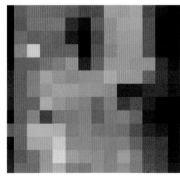

CLOSE UP before discarding pixels

AFTER PIXELS ARE DISCARDED, remaining ones are pushed together

UNIT 06.4

IMPROVING YOUR PHOTOGRAPHS →
SHARPENING UP

FUNDAMENTALLY, UNPROCESSED DIGITAL IMAGES REQUIRE SOFTWARE SHARPENING, OTHERWISE THEY WILL PRODUCE DISAPPOINTING RESULTS. WITHOUT SHARPENING, IMAGES WILL LACK CLARITY AND DEPTH.

Both digital cameras and scanners offer automatic sharpening filters, and these are often switched on by default. There is no way of reversing the effect on pre-sharpened images. It is much better to shoot and scan with all sharpening filters switched off, and to use the more precise tools in your image-editing application later. Then, if you go too far, you can always revert to an original version.

The Unsharp Mask Filter is the best tool for sharpening photographic scenes.

USING THE UNSHARP MASK FILTER (USM)

The Unsharp Mask Filter provides three modifiers: amount, radius, and threshold (strength, radius, and clipping in PaintShop Pro).

The radius (R) slider defines the number of pixels to adjust around each edge, the amount (A) slider defines the extent of contrast change, and the threshold (T) or clipping value is used to define the target difference between adjacent pixel lightness before sharpening is triggered. Each image will require its own individual interpretation, but as a starting point try the following setting:

■ Amount/strength: 100
■ Radius 1.0
■ Threshold/Clipping 1.0.

THE USM should be used with caution, but will give excellent results

UNSHARPENED

A:100, R:1 T1

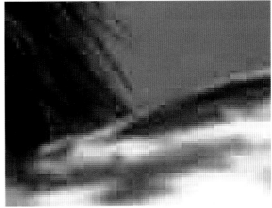

BLOCKY JPEG IMAGES . . .   . . . DO NOT SHARPEN WELL

KODAK PHOTO CD IMAGES All images scanned by Kodak and burned onto a Photo CD do need sharpening. Kodak uses a clever compression routine to cram high-resolution images into small data packets, but at the expense of sharpness. Use the USM filter before printing out for best results.

SHARPENING LOW-QUALITY JPEGS Coarse and blocky JPEG images are created by using too much compression and are beyond sharpening. To avoid this, apply a **Noise>Despeckle** filter before sharpening.

SHARPENING NOISY IMAGES Images that have been shot using high ISO settings such as 800 or 1600 will also contain a large proportion of randomly colored pixels called "noise." Fixed with a bright red or green color, noisy pixels will interfere with the sharpening process and become more visible. To avoid this, apply a Noise filter before sharpening.

IF YOU GO TOO FAR

Over-sharpened images have very contrasted edges and look almost like shallow carvings or reliefs. Remember, it is only necessary to tweak the image in order to make it print at maximum quality. If you are using it for the first time use your History palette to retrace your steps. You can also make a duplicate layer to sharpen rather than the original.

NOISY OR HIGH ISO SETTINGS . . .

A:100 R:3 T:1

A:150 R:6 T:1

. . . LOOK EVEN WORSE AFTER SHARPENING

UNIT 07.2

COLORING YOUR PHOTOGRAPHS →
GLOBAL COLOR CHANGE AND SEPIA

MAKING GLOBAL COLOR CHANGE IS JUST LIKE DIPPING A PHOTOGRAPHIC PRINT INTO A TRAY OF CHEMICAL TONER OR DYEING A PIECE OF FABRIC. THESE FOUR EXERCISES PRESENT SOME OF THE OPTIONS.

"WARMING" COLOR IMAGES

After shooting in less than perfect daylight or suffering the all too obvious effects of a flashgun, some images take on a bluish color and appear "cold." Psychologically, cold images are less attractive than warmer images to look at. In conventional photography, weak orange "warm-up" filters are often used to create a "sunlight" effect, but in digital photography you can do this in your software, without the extra expense of another camera gadget.

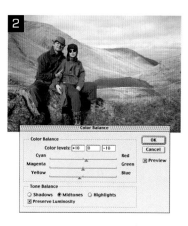

> **TIP**
>
> WARMING UP
> The trick with this command is keep a close watch on the neutral color areas in your image, such as skin tone or any mid-grays. Excessive color change will be most evident in these parts of your image.

1 Open the Color Balance dialog box and drag it away from your underlying image window, so you can see the effect your adjustments make.

2 Gently increase both Yellow and Red values until your image improves. Use no greater than a 20-point change in both cases.

STARTING POINT.

CHANGING COLOR TO BLACK-AND-WHITE OR MUTED TONES

Color images are created in the RGB color mode, just like shooting with color photographic film.

1 If you want to convert Red, Green, and Blue to Black and White, simply change the mode to Grayscale. As this process is so simple, there's never any reason to capture in Grayscale only.

2 If you want to give your image a muted color range, reduce the Saturation values in the Hue/Saturation dialog.

BLUE-TONED IMAGES

New color effects can also be created using the Color Balance sliders

1 Drain the image color away by changing to Grayscale mode, then change back again to RGB. You'll now be faced with a monochrome image in an RGB color space.

2 Select the Color Balance dialog and introduce new overall color by increasing Blue and Cyan. In the dialog box, work with the Midtones option checked first, then add other colors to the highlights by checking the Highlights option.

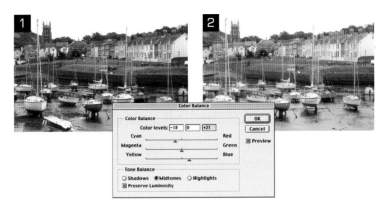

SEPIA IMAGES

There are many different ways to add an overall tone to your image, but using the Colorize command is by far the easiest and there's no need to change the image mode from RGB to Grayscale first.

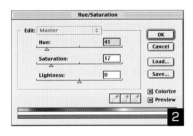

1 Make all your contrast and lightness corrections using the Levels adjuster, so you can see all image details in shadows and mid-tone areas.

2 Select the Hue/Saturation dialog and click on the Colorize option. This has the immediate effect of transforming your color image into a toned monochrome.

3 Use the Hue slider to pick the brown or sepia color and then follow this with the Saturation slider to determine its intensity. Low saturation settings produce the most subtle and delicate results.

OTHER PROGRAMS

PAINTSHOP PRO has identical Hue/Saturation and Color Balance controls.

MGI PHOTOSUITE users can experiment with Touch-up filters and the Sepia Flood tool.

TIP

SATURATION VALUES
Making radical color change is easy, but be wary of setting the saturation of your new color too high. Inkjet printers never print colors with the same intensity as seen on a monitor. Avoid increasing Saturation levels above +50.

UNIT 07.4

COLORING YOUR PHOTOGRAPHS →
MULTIPLE COLORING WITH COMMANDS AND SELECTIONS

THE MOST ADVANCED WAY TO CHANGE THE COLOR OF AN IMAGE IS TO USE COLOR CHANGE COMMANDS AND SELECTIONS TECHNIQUES.

USING ADJUSTMENT LAYERS

If you are undecided about committing to a color adjustment and would like the option of returning later on to change things around, then use an adjustment layer instead. Adjustment layers do not contain pixels in the conventional sense, only settings. Instead of choosing the Selective Color dialog, choose Layer>New Adjustment Layer and the Selective Color option. The same dialog box will appear and you can make an identical adjustment, but you will be able to return to the layer at a later stage to make changes. You can also cut holes into adjustment layers using the Eraser tool, allowing other underlying layers to show through.

TIP

PROBLEMS WITH AUTO SELECTION TOOLS
Auto tools like the Magic Wand or the Magnetic Lasso only work where there are consistent and adequate areas of color or contrast. The Magnetic lasso grips and locks onto the edges of image shapes that exhibit enough contrast. Manual selection will take more time to learn and refine, but will give you the best possible results.

USING SELECTIVE COLOR

Selecting is but one way of isolating a part of an image in order to make changes, but there is an easier way to change single dominant colors—using the Selective Color dialogue

1 Choose an image that has a large area of color that you'd like to alter. This could be a blue sky in a landscape or a vase of flowers.

2

3 Now try changing another color. Return to the Selective Color dialog and this time choose a different color, like yellow, from the pop-down menu. By increasing the quantity of black in your image and decreasing or draining out all the yellow, a totally different result is achieved.

3

2 Start by opening your image, then go to the **Image>Adjust>Selective Color** dialog box. Here you are given a drop-down menu that lists all the major colors, namely red, blue, green, cyan, magenta, and yellow. Choose Reds from the menu. Drag the dialog box to one side so you can see the effects on the whole image. Check the Preview button and experiment by moving the triangular sliders. Here, the magenta has been decreased and the yellow increased, but only in the red areas of the image. The result does not alter any other parts of the image.

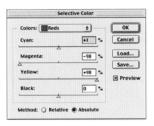

COLORING WITH GRADIENTS

You can easily mimic the look of a graduated camera filter used in conventional photography with the Gradient tool. This tool is useful for applying extra color to a sky.

1 Look for a landscape photo that needs a bit of extra coloring to make it a bit more visually interesting. The process works by making a seamless gradient of color from top to bottom, so make sure your image has a large sky area to work with.

2 Choose the Linear Gradient tool and set the Foreground Color to Transparency mode, with the Blending mode set to Color and the Opacity set to 60%.

3 Choose a color from your color picker. A deep orange is a good choice, as this will mimic the look of twilight or near sunset. If you want to intensify a weak blue sky, choose a strong blue instead. Now, place the Gradient tool at the top of your sky and click. Drag the line down and click once more to end the gradient. If it doesn't look right the first time, do **Edit>Undo** and repeat with a new gradient over a shorter distance.

1

3

UNIT 08.1

MIXING, MERGING, AND MONTAGE →
TOOLS

LIKE CUTTING OUT PHOTOS FROM A MAGAZINE AND PASTING THEM INTO A
NEW DESIGN OF YOUR OWN, MAKING A MONTAGE IS GREAT FUN BECAUSE
YOU DECIDE WHAT TO KEEP AND WHAT TO CUT.

TIP

FEATHERING
The extent of your feather value is related to
the overall pixel dimensions of your image. A
60-pixel feathered edge on a low-res 640 x
480 pixel image will dramatically increase the
size of your selection area. The same 60-pixel
feathered edge on a high-res 3000 x 2000
image will be hardly noticeable.

PRESET FEATHERING
You can pre-set all selection tools with a feather
value before you start using them. The only
disadvantage is that the pre-set remains until
you change it back to zero.

COPY AND PASTE

The Copy and Paste commands are common to all software
applications. A duplicate copy of a selected area or image is
transferred to an invisible part of your computer called the
Clipboard. It can then be pasted onto another document or image.
The Clipboard can only store one item at a time and is updated
each time you repeat the Edit>Copy command. The Edit>Paste
command brings the current contents of your clipboard back into
your work in progress.

LAYER ESSENTIALS

Layers are the best tool to use when starting montage projects,
as they can keep all elements separated. This example shows how
different layers are represented in the Layers palette and some of
the options available.

LAYERS ARE BEST USED for complex montage projects

LAYER BLENDS A blending mode is linked to the active layer only and determines how colors and contrast blend with the layer immediately underneath.

TEXT LAYERS Each time you use the Text tool, a new layer will be created automatically. A text layer is denoted by a T icon, meaning you can return to it at any time to change type size, color, and even correct spelling mistakes.

LINK/UNLINK ICON If you have two or more layers that should be grouped together for moving and transforming, you can link them. Click on one of the layers you want to use then go to the layer you want to link and click on the tiny blank box next to the Show/Hide icon until a tiny chain appears. To remove the connection, just click it again.

CHANGING LAYER ORDER All layers occupy their own position in a vertical stacking order. Uppermost and most visible is at the top of the palette with the base, or background layer at the bottom. You can alter the stacking order by dragging a layer icon upward or downward into a new position.

SHOW/HIDE ICON This tiny eye icon displays the contents of a layer when turned on. If you click and turn it off, the layer will become invisible, too. This is not the same as deleting a layer; it is used purely a visual aid.

LAYER OPACITY SLIDER This is used to determine the level of transparency of each individual layer in your project. Click on a layer you'd like to adjust and move the slider. At 100 percent a layer is completely opaque, obscuring everything underneath.

ADJUSTMENT LAYERS You can create non-pixel layers which "float" settings such as Levels, Color Balance, and Hue/Saturation over underlying layers. Click on the tiny white/black circle next to the New Layer icon and pick an option. Once the adjustment has been made, you can return and amend these as many times as you want.

CREATING, COPYING AND DELETING LAYERS To create a new empty layer, click on the tiny New Layer icon found at the bottom of the palette, next to the Wastebasket. This looks like a sheet of paper with one corner folded inward. An empty layer will be created immediately above the layer you were working on.

Besides creating new layers, existing ones can be duplicated. If you want to create an identical copy of a layer, click and drag the layer icon over the New Layer icon.

To delete a layer, click on the layer and drag it over the tiny wastebasket icon at the bottom right of the Layers palette (not the one on your desktop).

BACKGROUND LAYER Every digital image has a background layer, whether it has been created as a new file or imported from a digital camera or scanner. Unless you choose otherwise, all processing occurs on this layer. You can't cut transparent holes in the background layer or move its position in the vertical stacking order as long as the tiny layer lock icon is present. Any cuts will be filled automatically with the current background color. To get around this, double click on the background layer then rename it to Layer 0, or whichever name you choose.

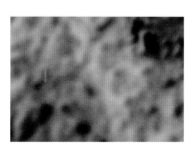

UNIT 08.2

MIXING, MERGING, AND MONTAGE
TEXT EFFECTS

UNLIKE PAINTING, DRAWING, AND WORD PROCESSING APPLICATIONS, YOUR IMAGING SOFTWARE ALLOWS YOU TO CREATE QUITE EXCITING TYPE. THIS PROJECT EXPERIMENTS WITH ALL THE MAJOR TYPE EFFECT TOOLS.

Montage—the digital combination of two or more separate images—forms the basis of much stunning advertising photography. To make a montage look totally convincing, you need to use your selecting tools to pick up the right area to transfer, then use brightness, contrast, and color balance to smooth away the differences. As in all digital projects, preparation and patience is the key to success.

 Difficulty > 3 or Intermediate
Time > less than 1 hour

VECTORS AND PIXELS

When first created, Type layers are constructed from vector shapes rather than square pixels. Vectors are like dot-to-dot puzzles, made from curved lines and nodes to create an outline shape. Type layers are separated from all of the pixel elements of your project and can be returned to for editing and even a spellcheck.

STARTING POINT

Chose a photo that has a large empty area or a large area of pattern. This will be used to place text into, so it needs to be free from clutter and distracting detail.

1 Click on the Type tool and generate a word. Increase the size of the type until it is visible and easy to read. Choose a type style that is solid and thick rather than one that looks like fine handwriting. Next choose a color that contrasts with the background elements to your image (otherwise it might be difficult to read clearly).

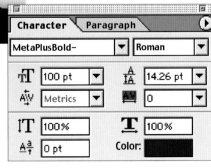

2 To blend solid color type with underlying detail, go to the Layers palette and click on the Type layer. Move the Opacity slider until the intensity of the original colors decreases. You can also experiment with Layer blends.

3 Sometimes the color of your type will need outlining to make it stand out more clearly from your background. Go to **Layers>Rasterize>Type** to convert your type to pixels. Select the letters by placing your cursor over their Layer icon, hold down Command/Ctrl then click. As the selection outline appears around each individual letter, you can now create the outline. From your color picker, choose a contrasting color, then **Edit>Stroke** and make a 10-pixel width command.

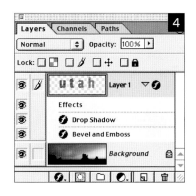

4 To fill type with pixels, choose the alternative Type tool, Type Mask, which is shown in the toolbox as an outlined T. This tool makes selection shapes out of letterforms that you can copy and paste or gradient fill. Click on your image and type a word. Notice how the dotted selection edges appear rather than a solid color letterform. **Edit>Copy**, then **Edit>Paste**, and watch how this creates a new layer. Pick your Move tool and drag this new text to another part of your image.

Version 5 Once you've used the Type Mask tool to make pixel filled type on a new layer, you can apply a range of creative edges to your letters. From the Layers menu, choose **Layer Effects>Drop Shadow**. Notice how a floating diffused edge now separates your type from the background details. There are many more Layer Effects to experiment with, such as Bevel and Emboss, and Inner Glow for creating 3-D type effects.

UNIT 08.3

MIXING, MERGING, AND MONTAGE →
TEXTURED AND TRANSLUCENT OVERLAYS

YOU CAN OVERLAY DIFFERENT DIGITAL IMAGES TO MAKE UNUSUAL AND ETHEREAL COMBINATIONS. BLENDING IMAGES TOGETHER IS A GOOD WAY TO GET RID OF UNWANTED BACKGROUNDS AND DETAILS.

i | **Difficulty** > 5 or Advanced
Time > more than 30 minutes

STARTING POINT

Scan in some sheets of paper textures such as wrapping paper or handmade papers that have been impregnated with flowers or leaves. These images will form the background for your project. Next photograph or scan some brightly colored flowers, making sure that you have plenty of different variations to use. Finally, scan in a favorite portrait. Open up one of your textured backgrounds, adjusting Color Balance and Levels as you would normally.

1 Open your portrait image, click **Edit>Select All,** then **Edit>Copy**. Click into your textured background image window, then select the **Edit>Paste** command. The portrait will now become a layer and part of your textured paper image. Close the portrait image window.

TIP

FASTER COPYING AND PASTING

 If you have two image windows on the desktop at the same time and you want to move a portion of one image to the other, simply make your selection, pick the Move tool then click drag the selection directly into the other image window. You won't be cutting out from the source image, only making a copy. The pasted section will automatically become a new layer.

■ If you want to transfer image elements that already exist as layers, you can simply click and drag individual layer icons into the destination image window. The result will be an identical layer copy.

2 Click on the portrait layer and pick the Eraser tool, set on Airbrush mode, with a soft-edged brush. Gently rub away all the unwanted edges, to reveal the underlying textures. If you are not confident, zoom in closer and use a smaller brush.

3 Apply a blending mode to this layer. Here, a Luminosity blend was used, allowing some of the paper texture to show through.

4 Open and **Edit>Copy>Edit>Paste** one of the flower images into your composition. Then erase all of the unwanted background.

5 Once perfect, duplicate the layers to make an additional version. Next, use the Move tool to arrange the position of the flower in each independent layer to overlap the portrait.

6 For each layer, adjust the Opacity slider so you can start to see underlying layers showing through. Make sure you activate a different layer each time. Finally, experiment with different blending modes, again for each layer separately.

Go through the blending options one by one, as it is impossible to predict the results of each.

7 Before printing out, save your work in the layer supporting Photoshop (.psd) file format. You'll notice that the size of the file increases with each image layer, so it's good practice to make and save a flattened version for printing purposes. From the tiny black triangle on the top right of the Layers palette pop-out menu, choose Flatten. This command compiles all separate layers into one and makes a leaner file for faster printing.

UNIT 08.4

MIXING, MERGING, AND MONTAGE →
MULTIPLE LAYERED LANDSCAPE

THERE IS NO REASON TO MAKE ALL YOUR DIGITAL PRINTS LOOK LIKE REAL PHOTOGRAPHS, AND WITH SO MANY TOOLS AT YOUR COMMAND, THE ONLY LIMIT IS YOUR IMAGINATION.

i **Difficulty** > 5 or Advanced
Time > more than 1 hour

STARTING POINT

Find an image that has plenty of empty space in the middle to place extra objects, such as a lake scene or a wide-angle landscape. You will also need a picture of a famous building, and a full-length portrait. Open your background image and make all the color and contrast adjustments as normal.

1 Open up the second image, and make a quick selection around the bits you want to paste onto the first. Use the Move tool to drag your selections into the landscape document. Use the Eraser tool, set with a large soft brush, to blend the edges. This reveals the underlying layer and lets the sand show through the end of the waterway.

TIP

PIVOTING AND ROTATING
You can access the Rotate command by the previous shortcut, but you need to place you cursor near the corner of the resize handles. In the center of the Rotate marquee is a tiny circle and this is the pivot point. Move this if you want to precisely shift your object around an axis other than its center.

 Making selections > go to pages 96-97

2

2 Remove the sky from around the building with the Magnetic Lasso selection tool then select **Edit>Cut**.

3 Open your third photograph. Make a selection, pick the Move tool, and drag it into your main image window. Use **Edit>Transform>Scale** until it's the right size. To prevent it from distorting, keep your finger on the Shift key. I decided to remove the flippers using the Eraser tool.

TIP

BETTER SELECTIONS
There's only one way to make razor sharp selections and that's by using the Pen tool. The Pen tool is used to lay down a series of interconnected nodes, a bit like a join-the-dots puzzle. These nodes can be repositioned and pulled and pushed into position to fit exactly around the object for cutting out. Once joined into a continuous loop a Path is created, viewed in its own Paths palette, which, in turn, can be converted into a selection.

PEN TOOL ESSENTIALS
■ Zoom into your image to at least 200 percent to get a good view of the pixel edge to your object.
■ Put the History palette on your desktop in case you need to retrace your steps.
■ Make nodes by clicking the Pen tool down with your mouse. To make a node with handles, click and drag your mouse. Handles are essential for describing arcs around curved shapes and can take a while to master.
■ Don't forget to save the Path, when finished, by double clicking on the Work Path icon in the Paths palette.

TRANSFORMING SHORTCUTS

Instead of using the drop-down menu, try using a keyboard short-cut. Command (Mac) Ctrl (PC) plus T, will give you the resize handle immediately. Keeping your fingers on both Option + Shift (Mac) or Alt + Shift (PC) lets you resize from the center outward or inward.

4 Next, you need to create a shadow to make the item you have just moved look convincing. In the Layers palette, place your cursor over the Boy layer icon and Command/Ctrl click to select it. Now, with the selection still on, make a new layer and **Edit>Fill** the selection with 100 percent black. If you can't see the black shadow, turn off the Boy layer.

5 With the black shadow still selected, select **Edit>Transform>Distort**. Drag each corner of the Transform box until it looks like the shadow is receding into the distance. Double click in the center to let it down, then finally adjust the Opacity slider for this black shadow layer to about 40 percent. This allows the sand to show through.

UNIT 09.1

CREATIVE EFFECTS → FILTERS

SOFTWARE FILTERS WORK IN EXACTLY THE SAME WAY AS SCREW-ON LENS FILTERS, BUT WITH A LOT MORE CREATIVE POSSIBILITIES.

This selection represents a choice of some of the most useful and fun filters. They are organized in sets, and you can control the intensity of each effect, making them as strong or subtle as you choose.

PIXEL

Pixel filters allow you to mimic the effects of photographic film grain or mosaic by breaking your images up into tiny fragments.

UNFILTERED

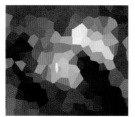
CRYSTALLIZE FILTER

MOSAIC FILTER

FILTERING IN SMALL AREAS

It is possible to filter selections, but a much better way to limit the effects of a filter is to make a duplicate layer, filter it, then cut away the unwanted areas with the Eraser. This means you have access to all the Layer variables such as opacity and blending modes.

ARTIST

With modifiers, like brush size, stroke length, and background texture, artist filters let you apply paint, pencil, and pastel effects to your images to give them a hand-rendered look. They often work well in simple, uncluttered still-life compositions and landscapes. Printing out on watercolor paper completes the effect.

UNFILTERED

SMUDGE STICK FILTER

WATERCOLOR FILTER

DISTORT

Distortion filters like Spherize, Wave, Twirl, and Ripple allow you to place an invisible "prism" over your image so you can distort things beyond your wildest dreams—great for mimicking the textures of metal and high-tech materials.

UNFILTERED

TWIRL FILTER

RIPPLE FILTER

TEXTURE

There is a wide range of textures that you can add to your images, from Canvas and Patchwork to Brick and Crackle.

UNFILTERED

CRACKLE FILTER

TEXTURIZER FILTER

BRUSHSTROKE

Like the Artist filters, the Brushstroke set gives you a variable range of paint application. Two filters worth trying are Spatter, which mimics the effect of thrown paint, and Sprayed Strokes, which looks like a dry brush dragged across wet paint.

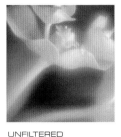
UNFILTERED

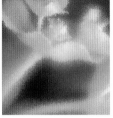
SPATTER FILTER

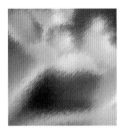
SPRAYED STROKES

FILTER FADING

To avoid an over obvious filter effect ruining your image, you can select the Edit>Fade Filter option immediately after making the filter command. Fade Filtering allows you to vary the opacity of the effect, just like the Layer opacity slider in your Layers palette. You can also choose blending modes.

WATERCOLOR FILTER (UNFADED)

FADED AT 50 PERCENT OPACITY
WITH LUMINOSITY BLENDING MODE

FILTERING TYPE

Because a Type layer is made from vectors, not pixels, you cannot apply a filter to it. To get around this, select Layer>Rasterize> Type. This changes the type layer into a pixel layer. Once complete you can apply any filter to it, but you will not be able to return and change the type face, font, or spelling. Blur filters can be used to great effect to make backgrounds for web graphics like buttons and banners. Take a brightly colored photograph and apply an all over Gaussian blur filter. Text can then be entered using the Type tool.

UNFILTERED

RASTERIZED, THEN FILTERED WITH
MOTION BLUR

BLUR

Blur filters are great for applying lens or camera movement effects. Gaussian Blur and Motion Blur are the most useful, and look good used with rendered type.

UNFILTERED

GAUSSIAN BLUR FILTER

MOTION BLUR FILTER

TROUBLESHOOTING

Working in an image mode other than RGB can cause filters to become grayed out and unavailable. If you have a CMYK mode image, most of the filter effects won't be available to you. If you are trying to edit a 48-bit image all of the filters will be out of use. Change back to 24-bit RGB. If the filters still don't work, check you are not trying to apply them to a Type layer.

UNIT 09.2

CREATIVE EFFECTS → MAKING
A WATERCOLOR PAINTING

LIKE ANY CAMERA FILTER, SOFTWARE FILTER EFFECTS SHOULD BE USED SPARINGLY AND ONLY IF THEY ACTUALLY IMPROVE AN ALREADY FANTASTIC IMAGE. USING EFFECTS FOR THE SAKE OF IT MAY MAKE YOUR IMAGES PREDICTABLE.

 Difficulty > 3 or Intermediate
Time > more than 30 minutes

 Making frames > go to pages 128–129

STARTING POINT

Find a landscape photograph that has all the elements of a good watercolor painting—preferably a scene with a dramatic sky and textural foreground. Try to avoid using photographs that have been overtly distorted by a wide-angle lens, as these may still retain the look and feel of a photograph even after a watercolor effect filter has been applied.

1 Open your image and make all the color and contrast adjustments as normal. Try and keep your image light, rather than dark and muddy, as this will help the filter to look its best.

2 Go to **Filters > Artistic > Watercolor** and modify the variables as shown.

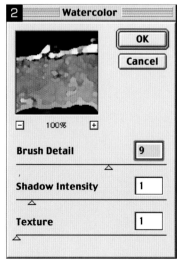

3 Wait for the filter to apply itself, and decide whether or not you are happy with the result. If not, **Edit > Undo** and try again with slightly different filter variables. If your result looks too heavy, reduce the Shadow Intensity slider. If there are not enough brush marks for you, increase the Brush Detail slider.

TIP

THE SMUDGE TOOL, shaped like a hand with a pointing finger, this lets you "pull" pixels from one area into another, just like running your finger through wet oil paint. This tool is great for merging contrasting image areas.

4 Once you are satisfied, save the image and put a watercolor edge on it using Extensis PhotoFrame, or if you don't have the software, PhotoFrame Online. Try and drag the edges into a complementary shape around the image.

5 If some of your colors look a bit pale and washed out, revive them using the Sponge tool, with a soft edges Airbrush, set on Saturate. Just try small areas, anything larger will ruin the washy watercolor effect.

OTHER PROGRAMS

PAINTSHOP PRO and MGI PHOTOSUITE users can both work with Extensis PhotoFrame online software for this project.

UNIT 09.4

CREATIVE EFFECTS → 3D RENDERING AND WARPING

PHOTOGRAPHS ARE NO LONGER CONFINED TO BEING FLAT AND TWO-DIMENSIONAL. YOU CAN EASILY "WRAP" AN IMAGE AROUND AN IMAGINARY SHAPE, BUT OTHER FACTORS WILL HELP IT LOOK CONVINCING.

STARTING POINT

In this project, we are going to make mini-earth globes from a white cloudy sky image, then arrange them to look like thought bubbles emerging from an unsuspecting friend. Choose a portrait photograph, a sky photograph, and a photograph of a pet. The sky image will be "wrapped" into a spherical shape to look like a miniature thought bubble containing your favorite pet.

1 Open up your portrait image and make sure there's enough space at the top of the frame to add the extra image elements. If you need to make more, pick the darkest tone from your image with the Eyedropper tool and set this to the background color. As you increase the Canvas size to make more space, it will be automatically created in this color.

2 Open any sky image and make color and contrast amendments where necessary. Use your Elliptical Marquee tool to draw a perfect circle, keeping your fingers on both the Shift and Alt keys when drawing. **Edit>Copy>Edit>Paste** this into a new layer.

3 From the Filters menu select **Distort>Spherize**. Set this to its maximum and watch your sky selection wrap itself into a sphere.

4 With the Move tool, drag this sphere layer into the portrait image. Don't resize it yet, as you'll need to paint some shadows and highlights on first. Just to be on the safe side, create a new layer to paint in, making sure it lies above the sphere layer in the Layers palette. Pick the Airbrush with a soft-edged brush set to Black and a low Pressure of around 20 percent. Select your sphere and start spraying black on the underside of the globe so it looks like shadow. Change the color to white and spray on the uppermost surface to create a highlight. Don't worry if your results are crude, because you can lower the opacity of the layers of this painting to blend things in.

TIP

THE EYEDROPPER TOOL
Instead of choosing a color at random from your color palette, use the Eyedropper tool to select or sample a color from within your image. This is a good way to guard against obvious and crude brushmarks.

CREATING "PERFECT" SQUARES AND CIRCLES
The Rectangular and Elliptical Marquee tools can be used in conjunction with your keyboard for more precise results. By holding down the Shift key, these tools will create a perfect square and circle respectively.

i **Difficulty** > 4 or Intermediate–Advanced
Time > more than 1 hour

OTHER PROGRAMS

MGI PHOTOSUITE has its own clever controls for 3-D rendering called Interactive Warp found under the Special Effects menu.

PAINTSHOP PRO has a huge number of 3-D effects to choose from. Use the Effects Browser for a visual preview beforehand.

5

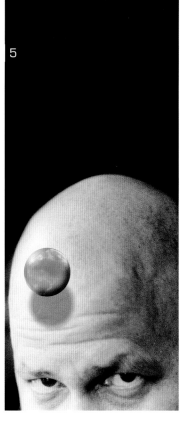

6

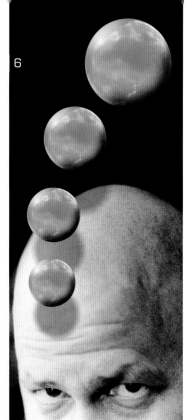

TIP

MOVING YOUR SELECTIONS
If your selection is created in the wrong place and
needs moving slightly, don't change over to the
Move tool. Keep your selection tool on, place your
cursor inside the selection area then drag iinto
place. If you do change to the Move tool, you'll
drag a selected part of the image by mistake.

8

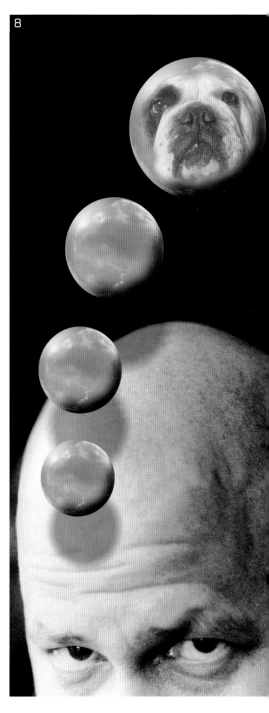

5 Once you are happy with the painting layer, merge it with the globe. You now need to make a shadow using the same selection. Create a new layer, **Edit>Fill** with black and apply a Gaussian Blur filter to make the blend. Drag this shadow to a point where it looks like it's lying under the globe layer like a natural shadow. Finally, change the shadow layer opacity until it blends with the person's forehead. Merge the globe and portrait layers together.

6 Once you have one perfect globe, just copy the layer for to make others. Make four in total and **Edit>Transform>Scale** to make them increasingly bigger. Drag them into position so that the shadows are overlapping each other to give the illusion of three-dimensional space.

7 Finally, open the image to fill the "thought bubble." Apply the same Distort filter to the face and then drag it into the main image. Use your eraser to remove any extra unwanted surrounding details.

8 The final result shows all elements combined together. The shadow below each bubble creates a convincing illusion of 3-D space.

7

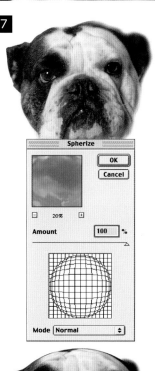

UNIT 10.1

PEOPLE AND PORTRAITS →
SELECTIONS

USING LAYERS IS ONE WAY OF MERGING OR ALTERING IMAGES, BUT SOMETIMES PRECISION SELECTION-MAKING IS CALLED FOR. THIS MAY APPLY TO ANY KIND OF IMAGE, BUT IS PARTICULARLY IMPORTANT FOR CONVINCING PORTRAITS.

MAKING SELECTIONS

As discussed in Unit 4.1, there are a variety of selection tools at your disposal (including the dotted Marquee tools, the freeform Pen or Lasoo, and the Magic Wand), and your choice will depend on what kind of selection you are making and which tool you feel more comfortable with. Very rarely can you draw a perfect selection outline in one attempt, and your project may contain elements that will be more easily selected using two or more selection tools. You can swap between the geometric Rectangular Marquee and the Lasso, providing you keep either Alt or Shift keys pressed down.

UNCONNECTED SELECTIONS Often, you might need to make simultaneous and unconnected selections in different parts of an image. Where the elements are different shapes and different colors, no one tool will capture them together. If you click outside a selection area at any time, this will immediately de-select it. If you want to make another unconnected selection area and include it in the previous selection, just keep your finger on the Shift key as you use the tool. A tiny "+" icon will appear next to the tool icon.

REMOVING A SELECTION

REMOVING A SELECTION FROM A SELECTION Sometimes you will need to remove an area from your selection, like excluding an eye from a selection of a person's face. Press down on the Alt key and watch a tiny "-" appear next to your selection tool. Now, use the tool to pick up the area for removal.

MAKING UNCONNECTED SELECTIONS can be a tricky process

INVERTING A SELECTION This technique has the opposite effect to defining a selection area, making everything other than the intended area into a selection. This is especially useful in situations where it is easier to select a similar colored background with the Magic Wand rather than a complex object full of different colors. After making your selection, **Select>Inverse**.

THE WHITE BACK-GROUND has been selected

SELECT>INVERSE selects everything but the white

THE SAVED SELECTION looks like a stencil

SAVING AND MOVING SELECTIONS

After a complex and time-consuming selection task, it is a good idea to save your hard work before moving it around.

SELECTIONS AROUND HAIRLINES The hardest kind of task is to make an accurate selection around a fringed edge, but the Extract command makes this easier. Found under **Edit>Extract**, this set of tools works by defining the edge with a highlighter pen, filling in the area you want to preserve, then deleting the rest.

SAVING Found under **Select>Save Selection**, any selection can be saved and stored as an invisible part of your image for future use. Once saved, selections are found in the Channels palette and look like simple black or white stencils. To retrieve a saved selection, simply **Select>Load Selection**.

MOVING You can easily move a selection within an image, or from one image to another. Place two or more image documents side-by-side on your desktop and make a selection in one of them. Keep the selection tool on and place your cursor inside the selection shape, then drag it into the other image document. Moving a selection from an image will leave a selection-shaped "hole."

HAIRLINES ARE particularly difficult to cut around.

THE EXTRACT TOOL simplifies the time-consuming task of complex selections

UNIT 10.3

PEOPLE AND PORTRAITS →
COLORING EFFECTS

COLORING GIVES YOU A GREAT OPPORTUNITY TO HAVE TOTAL CONTROL OVER YOUR PORTRAITS, ESPECIALLY IF THEY WERE THE WRONG COLOR TO START WITH. THESE TWO QUICK PROJECTS INVOLVE DESATURATION, TINTING, AND CHANGING THE DOMINANT COLOR.

i **Difficulty** > 3 or Intermediate
Time > less than 30 minutes

STARTING POINT

Open a well-exposed color image that would benefit from a more subtle color effect. This photograph was shot in warm daylight, but to give it a softer effect we can drain the colors away and then put some, but not all, back.

1 Choose **Layer>Duplicate Layer** so that there are two identical layers lying over each other.

2 Click on the uppermost layer to make it active and then from the **Image> Adjust** menu, choose Hue/Saturation. Using the Saturation slider, drain the color away, moving the slider to about -75.

3 Return to your image and notice how the overall color has disappeared from the uppermost layer, but remains fully in the background layer

STARTING POINT

Sometimes a background color or the color of a garment totally ruins a great picture. Rather than make a painstaking selection around the offending area, use the Selective or Replace Color controls for an easier fix. Choose an image with a solid color area that you'd like to change, such as a car or an article of clothing. This example shows a dull blue wall which will be changed to bright purple.

1 Open up your image and identify the color you want to change. It does not need to be in one enclosed area; the command will pick it all up like a magnet. For this image, I am going to change the background color.

2 From the Image menu, select **Adjust> Replace Color**. This dialog presents you with a blacked out preview window at first, and then the Dropper tool will appear. Drag it down on the color you want to change. Now notice the white areas appearing in the dialog. Whatever is white will be selected for changing. You can expand or contract this by moving the Fuzziness slider at the top of the dialog.

3 Remaining in the Replace Color dialog, move the Hue slider until you find a new color that suits.

4 Using the Eraser tool, set to Airbrush mode, use a very low Pressure such as 3 percent. Zoom into the parts of the image you want to change and gently rub them away. Take care to not overdo the erasing, or you'll end up with colors that are too strong emerging from the layer underneath. If you make a mistake, delete the layer, make another background duplicate, and start again.

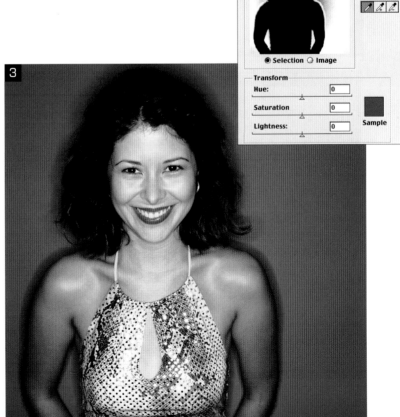

UNIT 11.2

LANDSCAPES AND PLACES →
TURNING DAY INTO NIGHT

YOU CAN EASILY TRANSFORM LATE AFTERNOON OR TWILIGHT PHOTOGRAPHS INTO SHOTS THAT LOOK LIKE THEY WERE TAKEN AT NIGHTFALL.

 Difficulty > 3 or Intermediate
Time > 1.5 hours

 Making selections > go to pages 96-97

By using carefully drawn selections you can drape nightfall over certain parts of your image, rather than over the whole scene, and thus create a very distinctive result. Natural light produces a range of colors during daylight hours, but you can still manipulate skies to look like night has fallen.

STARTING POINT

Pick a landscape shot that was taken in late afternoon and that has good portions of both sky and water, as the effect will look most dramatic in these areas. The scene in the image below is already showing some evening color in the pale violet of the sky and the first signs of an orange-tinted sunset. At this stage, retouch any blemishes if necessary using your Rubber Stamp tool.

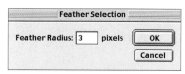

THE MAGNETIC LASSO

If you are finding it difficult to make an accurate selection using the Magic Wand tool, try using the Magnetic Lasso. This works by "searching" for a contrasting edge between pixels then laying down a selection line. It won't create a line between similar colored areas.

1 First, isolate the sky by making a selection with the Magic Wand tool. The sky will not be uniform in color or regular in shape, so you will need to keep refining your selection as you work. Use the Shift or Alt keys to add or take away pixels from your selection. Take time to make as accurate a selection as you can, as sloppy work will be very visible later. Soften your selection with a feathered edge by choosing **Select>Feather** from the drop down menu. Apply a 3-pixel Feather radius.

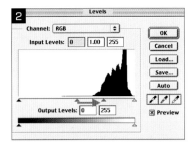

2 To make the sky darker, apply a Levels command. You have already selected part of the image, so any command you make at this stage will be restricted to that fenced-off selection area. Go to **Image>Adjust>Levels** and, instead of dragging the midtone slider to the left, drag it to the right side to make the sky darker. Don't push it too far in one go or it will look too dark.

3 Repeat steps 2 and 3 in the water area of your image, making sure you draw a careful and precise selection. Make this part of your photo much darker than the sky as it will help to direct emphasis.

4 Finally, return to the sky area and introduce some additional color by using your Sponge tool. Instead of choosing a color at random from the color picker or even from the image itself, set the Sponge tool on Saturate mode. Pick a soft-edged brush and drag the brush over the sky to intensify all the colors underneath.

ADDING COLOR

Don't worry if your starter image doesn't contain the pinkish reds of late afternoon: you can introduce them using your Color Balance controls. After Step 2, go to Image>Adjust>Color Balance and check the Highlight option. Increase the amount of Red and Yellow until it looks right.

DARK PRINTS

If your prints from this project are turning out too dark, then you may have overdone it with your nighttime effects. Printers are not good at reproducing near-shadow tones, so you'll need to lighten your image to make amends. Go to the Levels dialog and push the midtone slider to the left.

UNIT 11.4

LANDSCAPES AND PLACES →
REFLECTIONS AND WATER

IN THIS PROJECT WE WILL INSERT A SHALLOW STRETCH OF WATER IN FRONT OF AN HISTORIC BUILDING, CREATE A REFLECTION FROM THE BUILDING ITSELF, AND THEN MERGE THE TWO TOGETHER.

i | **Difficulty** > 4 or Intermediate–Advanced
Time > 1.5 hours

STARTING POINT

You'll need to find photographs of an historic building and a watery landscape.

1 Open the image of the building and free up some space in the foreground for your montage. Use your Rubber Stamp tool to remove any unwanted elements. This image has a tiled foreground with a recognizable diminishing perspective shape, plus a useful texture to show through the water.

2 Open your landscape image and select **Edit>Select All>Copy**. Close this image and select **Edit>Paste** to paste it into the building image.

3 After pasting, use the Eraser tool set with a soft-edged brush to blend the water with the underlying tiles. This will remove all the hard edges and reveal some of the underlying walkway detail.

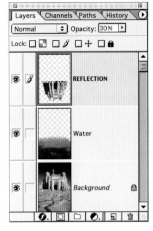

THE LAYERS PALETTE

4 To further blend the water with the walkway, click on the water layer and reduce its opacity to 80 percent. The underlying detail will now show through, but the water still remains recognizable and retains its strong blue color.

5 Turn the water layer off, then click on the background layer and make a selection of the building. There's no need to make a precise selection at this stage as most of the surroundings can be removed after the next stage. Click **Edit>Copy** and **Edit>Paste** to bring a copy of your building into a new layer. Next, from the Edit menu select **Transform>Flip Vertical**. This will rotate the piece into the right upside-down position.

6 Drag the upside-down building into place and then change its perspective to make it look as if it is diminishing in the distance. Select the reflection, then from the Edit menu, choose **Transform>Perspective**. Drag one of the corner handles nearest the bottom of the image toward the center to squeeze the reflection into the right shape. Finally, remove excess blue sky by using the Magic Wand and **Edit>Cut**.

7 Return to your Layers palette and turn the water layer back on. Adjust the reflection layer's opacity to around 30 percent so that it blends into the water.

Unit 12: Printing out

12.1 How printers work   114
12.2 Print media   116
12.3 Frequently asked questions   118
12.4 Using online photo labs   120

Unit 13: Creative print projects

13.1 Tools   122
13.2 Using art papers   124
13.3 Panoramas   126
13.4 Making frames   128

Unit 14 Preparing photos for email and the Internet

14.1 Shrinking   130
14.2 Sending images as attachments   132
14.3 Web galleries   134

PRINT AND PUBLICATION

UNIT 12.1

PRINTING OUT → HOW PRINTERS WORK

WITH THE ENORMOUS RANGE OF DIGITAL PRINTING DEVICES TO CHOOSE FROM, HOW DO YOU KNOW WHICH KIND GIVES THE BEST RESULTS?

INKJET PRINTERS

In a process similar to that by which color photographs are reproduced in books and magazines, an inkjet printer uses tiny dots to create the illusion of color. Each color inkjet printer uses four to six colors of ink to assemble a print from millions of minute dots that are different sizes and distances from one another. These tiny dots are arranged by the printer and merged by the human eye to create a convincing representation of photographic color.

After your imaging software, the factor with the greatest bearing on the quality of your final output is the printer's own dedicated software. Along with familiar settings like paper size and print quantity, an inkjet has numerous preset options for selecting different media types, such as glossy or matte paper, or film. It is essential to adjust the printer settings to suit your intended media, as they instruct the printer on how much ink to spray and how far apart to place the dots. Using a given setting on the wrong media type will give disappointing results.

CLOSE UP an inkjet print is made from millions of tiny overlapping ink dots

THE HOME INKJET Available at low cost and designed principally for a range of family uses, the most basic inkjet uses three colors: cyan, yellow, and magenta (CMY) plus black (called K to avoid confusion with blue). The home inkjet gives good results for printing reports and school projects, but falls short when it comes to mimicking the delicate colors in a photograph. The four-color model will show obvious dots in what are supposed to be blank highlight areas of an image.

A HOME/OFFICE INKJET PRINTER

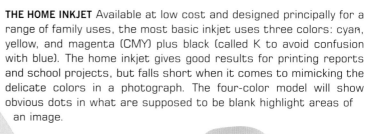

A FOUR-INK COLOR INKJET

THE PHOTO QUALITY INKJET As the word "photo" on the product packaging indicates, this type of device gives much better results. than a home inkjet. At around twice the cost, this printer uses the same CMYK color set, plus two additional inks, light cyan and light magenta. The addition of these extra colors allows for a more accurate rendition of flesh tones and subtle photographic colors. It also makes the dots less obtrusive. To get more for your money, opt for a printer that uses lightfast or pigment inks, such as an Epson Stylus Photo with "Intellidge" ink cartridges. The manufacturers claim that the lifespan of such prints is extended by up to 100 years.

THE PROFESSIONAL INKJET Sold at about three times the cost of a photo quality inkjet, these printers are aimed largely at professional photographers and designers. The device can spray ink at very high resolutions (between 1440 and 2880 dpi), making its output virtually indistinguishable from traditional photographic prints. By using lightfast or pigment inks with this kind of printer you can make long-lasting and archival quality prints, albeit at a higher cost for ink cartridges and purpose-made papers. Pigment printers are not able to reproduce very saturated colors and produce less vivid prints than ink-based inkjets.

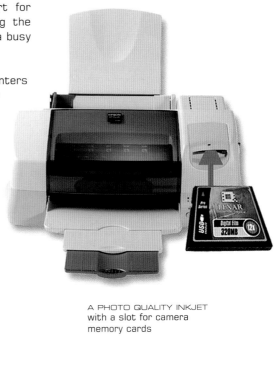

A PROFESSIONAL INKJET
using pigment inks

CARD READER PRINTERS Some printers have a built-in port for printing directly from digital camera memory cards. Using the printer's preset software, good results can be achieved in a busy office or out on location without the need for a computer.

BANNER PRINTING AND PANORAMIC PAPER Most good-quality printers have a roll paper adapter or can accept custom-size paper lengths of up to 30 inches (76cm), so you can make banner prints on long strips of paper. The only limitation is the width of the printer carriage.

A PHOTO QUALITY INKJET
with a slot for camera
memory cards

A PHOTO QUALITY INKJET
fitted with a roll paper adaptor

UNIT 12.2

PRINTING OUT → PRINT MEDIA

ONE OF THE BEST THINGS ABOUT AN INKJET PRINTER IS THE HUGE VARIETY OF DIFFERENT MEDIA ON WHICH THEY CAN PRINT. UNLIKE TRADITIONAL PHOTOGRAPHIC PRINTING, YOU CAN USE YOUR INKJET TO PRINT ON CANVAS, WATERCOLOR PAPER, AND OTHER TEXTURED MEDIA.

EPSON AND CANON BRAND MEDIA

Designed to produce top quality results when used in conjunction with their own inks and printers, these papers are an ideal starting point for a new user.

Working out an accurate product description from a packet of inkjet paper can be far from straightforward, but here's a rundown of the most popular types.

PAPER SIZES

The International Standards Organization (ISO) has determined a universal set of paper for printing and stationery called the A scale.

A0	**33⅛ x 46¹³⁄₁₆ in**
A1	**23⅜ x 33⅛ in**
A2	**16½ x 23⅜ in**
A3	**11¹¹⁄₁₆ x 16½ in**
A4	**8¼ x 11¹¹⁄₁₆ in**
A5	**5¹³⁄₁₆ x 8¼ in**

In the USA it is still more common to use the scale based on traditional office machinery, with sizes as follows:

Executive	**7¼ x 10½ in**
Folio	**8¼ x 13 in**
Foolscap	**8 x 13 in**
Legal	**8½ x 14 in**
Letter	**8½ x 11 in**
Statement	**5½ x 8½ in**

INKJETMALL.COM
If you want to find out more about the most highly regarded brands of media, try visiting the Inkjetmall web site. This site offers impartial and independent reviews of all kinds of media and techniques to get the best out of your printer. Go to **www.inkjetmall.com**.

Canon

PRO

- *Professional Photo Paper for the highest quality digital photographic output*
- *Papier Photo Professionnel pour la qualité optimale des impressions photos numériques*
- *Professional Photo Paper für höchste Qualität im digitalen Fotodruck*
- *Papel fotográfico profesional para impresiones de alta calidad digital*
- *Professional Photo Paper, per il migliore risultato di qualità fotografica digitale*
- *Professioneel foto papier voor de hoogste kwaliteit in digitale fotografische afdruk*

For/Pour/Für/Para/Per/Voor:
BJC-8200 *Photo*

Photo Paper Pro
Papier Photo Professionnel / Professional Fotopapier
Papel Fotográfico Profesional / Carta Fotografica Professionale
Professioneel Fotopapier
PR-101
A4 |15 Sheets / Feuilles / Blatt / Hojas / Fogli / Vel

DESPITE THEIR HIGHER COST, Epson and Canon papers should help you to get maximum quality results from your printer

STANDARD INKJET PAPER Available cheaply and in huge packets of up to 500 or 1000 sheets, standard inkjet paper is obtainable from most office supply stores. With a smooth, matte surface, this paper is only really suitable for printing text and graphics. It is often called 360 dpi paper.

PHOTO PAPER Photo paper is thicker than standard paper, is considerably more expensive, and has a matte finish. The paper is coated with a thin layer of finely powdered clay, which helps it hold tiny ink dots in place and reproduce color better than 360 dpi paper. Photo paper is available in all popular sizes and thicknesses, and some types are double-sided. It is sold under the major photographic brand names, including Epson, Kodak, and Canon.

GLOSSY PHOTO PAPER Like its matte counterpart, glossy photo paper is best for six-color inkjet printers. Glossy papers have a smooth and shiny surface that reproduces saturated colors well over a wide tonal range. Glossy papers print deeper blacks than matte papers, but thinner paper weights will crease easily. They are available in all popular sizes, but are single-sided only.

PREMIUM OR PHOTO-WEIGHT GLOSSY PAPER This is a much thicker glossy paper, specifically designed to resemble conventional resin-coated photographic paper. With a more substantial feel than normal-weight glossy, and much improved resistance to creasing, this kind of media is best suited to occasions when frequent handling is inevitable. It is made by many traditional photo paper manufacturers, including Ilford and Kodak.

GLOSSY PHOTO FILM This is a plastic material, impossible to rip by hand, that evokes the most sharply detailed results from your printer. Sheets are single-sided and cannot be folded.

PURPOSE-MADE INKJET ART MEDIA Without the "plasticky" surface of glossy photo papers, inkjet art papers represent a more tactile choice of media. The best brands are Somerset and Lyson, both of which permit fine detail and saturation with texture. Very heavy weights, of up to 120 lbs (250gsm), are available.

ARTISTS' WATERCOLOR PAPER Although seemingly identical to purpose-made inkjet media, artists' watercolor paper can give unpredictable results with an inkjet. The best papers to use are the most expensive types used for artists' lithographs and screenprinting, such as Rives and Fabriano, sold by the sheet rather than in sketchbooks. These are great for creating deckled or ripped edges.

TRANSFER AND OVERHEAD PROJECTOR ACETATES Colorless plastic films can be used to make presentation slides for projection or self-adhesive jobs. One side of the media has a slightly granular feel, which helps it to accept the ink. It will not reproduce vivid colors in the way that photographic display transparency film does.

ARCHIVAL PAPER is best used for printing photos that are on continuous display in a picture frame

SOMERSET ENHANCED PAPERS have gained a reputation as the professional's favorite media

GLOSSY PAPER is the best all-round media for high-quality photographs

CANVAS CLOTH INKJET media adds a rich texture to your prints

UNIT 12.3

PRINTING OUT → FREQUENTLY ASKED QUESTIONS

THE FINAL STEP—PRINTING OUT YOUR WORK—CAN BE PROBLEMATIC AND FRUSTRATING UNLESS YOU KNOW THE FOLLOWING SOLUTIONS.

THE PHOTO ON THE LEFT simulates the image previewed on a monitor. On the right is the duller printed version.

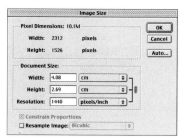

THERE'S NO NEED to have the Resolution set as high as 1440 dpi, 200 dpi will be more than adequate

INDIVIDUAL INK DOTS surrounded by white space means you've probably selected a low-quality print option

Q. My printouts never have the same rich colors as those shown on my monitor. What am I doing wrong?

A. Printers use a much smaller color palette than monitors. This is because they mix their colors using CMYK rather than RGB ingredients. If you use Photoshop, try switching the Gamut warning on to see which colors won't print out, or the View Proof command to see a simulation of the likely printout.

Q. I have a1440-dpi inkjet. Does that mean I have to prepare my image files at a 1440-dpi resolution to get the best results?

A. No, despite anything you read on a product's packaging, the real resolution of a six-color 1440 printer is around 240 dpi. This figure is arrived at by dividing 1440 by the number of different colors used. In practice, if you make your image files 200 dpi, you'll always get top quality.

Q. Why do my printouts look speckled and coarse even though I'm using a high-resolution image file to print from?

A. Your printer can be set to print at various different qualities described as draft, high, and photo, or by the actual number of ink dots, for example 360, 720, or 1440. These are often selected for you when you choose a particular type of media. Choose a higher setting in your printer dialog box and reprint the image.

Q. Why do my printouts show very obvious square blocks even though I'm using my printer with its highest 1440-dpi setting?

A. Only one thing causes blocky printouts: a low-resolution image. At a resolution of 72 dpi, pixels are clearly visible and will appear as jagged edges or blocks in your prints. Images set to 200 dpi have tiny pixels that are invisible to the naked eye. Either reprint at a smaller size, or reshoot/ rescan at a higher resolution.

BLOCKY PRINTS mean only one thing: a low-resolution original

Q. Why do images that I've downloaded from the Internet always print out-of-focus?

A. All images used on the Internet are set with a 72-dpi resolution. If you try and enlarge them for printing out you'll see a drastic loss of sharpness because there are more interpolated (or "invented") pixels than original ones.

Q. My recent printouts have an all-over yellow cast, which is still present after I've tried a Color Balance adjustment. How can I fix this?

A. Either your ink cartridge has run out of one or more colors, or it has a blocked nozzle. As ink runs out or is prevented from reaching the paper, the color mix on paper becomes very unpredictable. Use the printer software to clean the printer heads and, if that doesn't work, change your color cartridge and reprint.

IF YOU OVER-ENLARGE a low-resolution image, it will lose sharpness

WILDLY INCORRECT COLOR suggests an ink-flow problem

Q. Why do my prints look dark and soggy when I use artists' papers?

A. Artists' papers are not designed to hold tiny individual ink dots in place. Instead they merge and run into each other much like ink on blotting paper. To get the best results out of this type of media, make your image brighter than normal and use your printer at its lowest setting, such as 360 dpi or draft.

ARTISTS' PAPERS are not designed to cope with inkjet printing and can "flood" if your image is on the dark side

UNIT 12.4

PRINTING OUT → USING ONLINE PHOTO LABS

THE LATEST INNOVATION IN PRINTING DIGITAL IMAGES IS THE ONLINE PHOTO LAB. IF YOU HAVE AN INTERNET CONNECTION AND ARE FAMILIAR WITH A WEB BROWSER, THE REST IS EASY.

PHOTO LAB URLS

www.fotowire.com
www.ofoto.com
www.fotango.co.uk
www.photobox.co.uk
www.colormailer.com

HOW IT WORKS

Connected to the web server is an automated mini-lab printer, like the ones used in a regular downtown processing shop. Your files are automatically transferred to the mini-lab without any human intervention, day or night. Digital mini-labs, like the Fuji Frontier, use a fine laser to project images onto conventional photo paper at a very low cost. Because no lens is used, there is no sign of scratchy dust or slipping focus errors on your prints. Such high quality has to be seen to be believed.

PHOTOLABS deliver very high-quality results and make family snapshots look their best

UPLOAD SOFTWARE

Most Internet photo labs can be reached via the two popular web browsers, Internet Explorer and Netscape Communicator, on both PC and Mac platforms. Some labs use their own specially designed upload software, such as the ColorMailer Photo Service 3.0. This application is freely available from their web site and provides a better range of useful tools than either of the browsers. Different from all other services, the ColorMailer Photo Service software allows you to crop your images, choose borders and, most importantly, tells you when your order exceeds the quality of your file. ColorMailer, like Kodak, has labs across all continents, so you can pick a destination to upload to and benefit from the local postage service when sending prints to overseas friends—and it takes a fraction of the time.

COMPRESSION AND TRANSFER TIME

Sending image files over the Internet can take a long time, and the larger your image files are, the longer they will take to transfer. The obvious temptation is to compress image data for a faster (and cheaper) upload, but the resulting prints will lose quality. Save images for print-out in the JPEG format, but only use highest quality settings such as 8–10 or 80–100 percent. Prepare your images at 200 dpi if you want to avoid visible pixelation on your results.

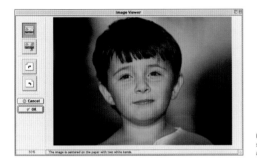

COLORMAILER UPLOAD software allows you resize and rotate your images

STORAGE AND SHARING YOUR IMAGES

AN INTERNET-BASED photo lab offers a wide range of printing and storage services, plus facilities for sharing your work with friends

Most Internet photo labs also provide a password-protected storage area so you can keep your images safely on a remote server. There are many different services available, but most labs charge extra for this option. Some offer storage free for a limited time and others delete your work after the free period has elapsed. The advantage of paying for a service like this is that you can share a password-protected photo album with friends across the world. They are able to place their own print orders direct, without costing you a penny.

ONCE YOU'VE CHOSEN an image for printing, you get a larger on-screen version to check first

MANY LABS let you catalog and organize your photos into sets. This service displays all the images from one upload in miniature so you can see them all together.

UNIT 13.1

CREATIVE PRINT PROJECTS → TOOLS

YOUR SOFTWARE CAN BE USED TO CREATE A WIDE RANGE OF DIFFERENT PRINT EFFECTS, FROM TONING AND SHARPENING TO ADDING CAPTIONS, AND PREVIEW TOOLS GIVE A GOOD IDEA OF THE END RESULT.

PRINT PREVIEW

OTHER PROGRAMS

PaintShop Pro has a very simple File>Print Preview function which displays a full-screen prediction of the image on your chosen paper.

MGI PhotoSuite users can also use a print preview function together with a Nudging option for repositioning the image on the print paper.

It can be difficult to know just how big an image will print on paper, and this is where a preview tool such as the one found in Photoshop packages comes in handy. Clicking into the Document tab, found at the bottom left corner of your image window, causes a tiny preview window to pop up. The outer square shows the current paper size and the inner square shows the size at which your images will print. If the image is too small, go back to the Image Size dialog box and check that the Resolution isn't set too high. With the Resample button unchecked, change the resolution to 200 dpi. Recheck the print preview to see a bigger inner square.

If the inner square overlaps the outer square, then your image is too big for the paper currently selected. Either choose a bigger paper size or go back to your Image Size dialog and check the present settings. If your image resolution is set to 72 dpi, uncheck the resample button and change to 200 dpi. This will make a smaller printout. If it's still too big, you need to downsize your image and throw away some pixels. Return to the Image Size dialog, select the Resample button and make the current Document Size smaller than your paper.

You can also use your printer software to print an image at less then 100 percent. However, the exact percentage reduction is a little tricky and it will also take a lot longer to process and print the image.

THIS TINY PREVIEW, bottom left corner, shows how your photo will be positioned

THIS PREVIEW INDICATES that your image will print very small

IF YOUR IMAGE is too large to fit on the paper, the preview will look like this

PRINTER SOFTWARE PRESETS

All printer software is supplied with various options for adjusting color, tone, and sharpness, and adding effects like sepia. These options are designed for users who don't have any imaging software to process their digital camera files. Presets do a good job of printing raw digital camera files, but give you much less control than a good software package like PaintShop Pro or Photoshop Elements. If you want to be in total control of your printouts, make sure all presets are turned off before making a print. Some digital cameras can be connected directly to a printer and some printers have slots that accept digital camera memory cards. Preset effects are an ideal way to make good quality prints in these circumstances.

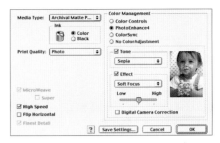

PRINTER SOFTWARE preset commands override the precise controls used in your imaging application and should not be used for critical work

PRINT CAPTION

Photoshop and Photoshop Elements users have a largely hidden dialog box for adding captions to their images. Found under **File>Info**, you have the option of typing a descriptive caption. Once the image is saved, the caption remains hidden but can be called up when the Print Caption option is selected in your printer software. Provided there is blank space between the edge of your image and the edge of the printing paper, the caption will be placed along the bottom edge using a default Helvetica or Arial typeface.

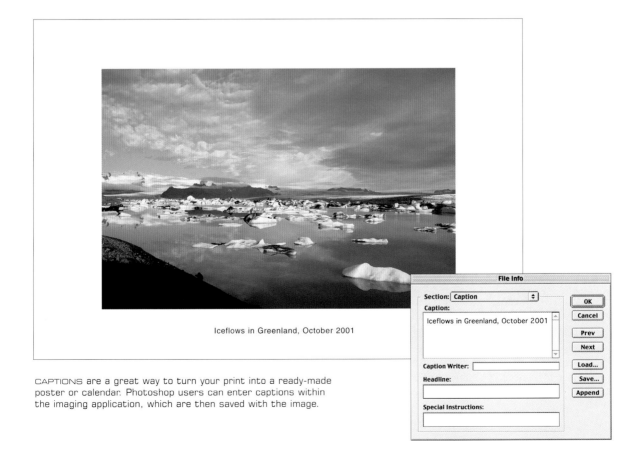

Iceflows in Greenland, October 2001

CAPTIONS are a great way to turn your print into a ready-made poster or calendar. Photoshop users can enter captions within the imaging application, which are then saved with the image.

UNIT 13.2

CREATIVE PRINT PROJECTS → USING ART PAPERS

TEXTURED ARTISTS' PAPERS ALLOW YOU TO CREATE A KIND OF HYBRID PHOTOGRAPH/PAINTING. ALWAYS START OFF WITH YOUR PRINTER'S LOWEST QUALITY OUTPUT SETTING, OFTEN CALLED DRAFT OR NORMAL.

MAKING A TEST PRINT

One important preliminary when using non-standard media is to print a test strip. Adopted from a darkroom technique of the same name, a test print is used to judge exposure and color balance before printing on, and possibly wasting, a full-size sheet of paper.

1 First pick the rectangular Marquee from your toolbox and make a selection of the area you want to test. On a portrait, it should include an area of skin tone, but on other images it should include both shadow and highlight areas.

2 Under **File>Print**, check **Print Selected Area**, and choose the paper size, then print. Your selection will be printed on the paper ready to assess. Notice how the color balance varies with print brightness on the three color tests.

TOO LIGHT

CORRECT PRINT

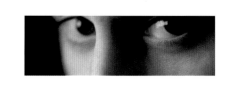

TOO DARK

MAKING CARDS AND BOOKLETS

There are several different ways to position your image on your printing paper, made easier with the latest versions of Photoshop and Photoshop Elements. Basic positioning is limited to Central in the Portrait or Landscape formats, but better tools allow you to specify borders, and drag and drop.

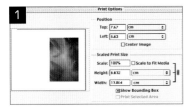

2 If you are printing on paper that will be folded like a greeting card or booklet, keep the fold in mind when positioning your images. Remember, if you want to print on both sides of a sheet of paper, that the second image should be inverted before printing.

1 In Photoshop choose **File>Print Options** and select **Show Bounding Box**. Now deselect **Center Image** and move your cursor over the image icon. Drag the image into position on any part of your paper area, using the position indicators if you want to be exact.

*Good Luck
in your
new job*

USING SKETCHPAD PAPERS

Not all artists' papers are suitable for inkjet printing due to an invisible coating called "size," originally designed to stop watercolor paint spreading. Papers vary in their type and size—from blotting paper, which has no size at all, to rigid watercolor pad paper, which usually has a thick coating. If the ink on your watercolor paper prints puddles on the surface, try a cheaper cartridge paper for better results.

WRITING PAPERS

Common bond or laid writing papers give excellent results with inkjet printers, especially if they have a texture and watermark. When preparing your image files, use your Levels mid-tone slider to make the image much brighter than normal and combine this with the lowest quality printer setting, such as Draft or 360 dpi. These papers are usually quite thin and will get soggy if you try and print out edge to edge. Only make small prints on this type of media.

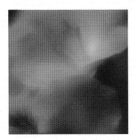

PRINTING ON CUSTOM PAPER SIZES

You don't always have to print out on A4 or Letter-sized paper—you can set your printer to recognize your own custom shapes. Cut some sheets of paper down into panoramic aspect ratios and measure them with a ruler. Next, open your printer software and select the Custom option. Create a name for your paper and enter its dimensions when prompted. Once saved, this will always appear in the same pop-up Paper Size menu as standard sizes such as A4, A3, and so on. When you preview the image, your custom size will appear too.

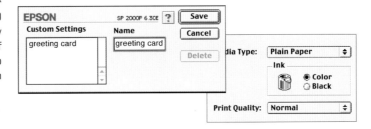

RIPPED OR DECKLED EDGES

Don't rip paper before printing, as the fibers could clog up your printer's inkjet nozzles. Print on oversize paper and then rip into shape once the print has dried. For deckled edges, gently score and fold the paper first before tearing slowly by hand. Good-quality artists' paper with a weight above 100 lbs (200 gsm) will rip nicely.

UNIT 13.3

CREATIVE PRINT PROJECTS →

PANORAMAS

THERE ARE MANY SOFTWARE TOOLS YOU CAN USE TO "STITCH" SEPARATE
IMAGES INTO A PANORAMIC SHOT VIEW FOR WEB OR PRINT OUTPUT.

Difficulty > 2 or Easy/Intermediate
Time > 1 hr

Spin Panorama is included, free of charge, with all latest Epson
inkjet printers, and offers a precise set of tools for joining different
frames together. PhotoImpact and MGI PhotoSuite both have built-
in panorama options. The most advanced software package, Quick
Time Virtual Reality Studio, is made by Apple. All applications give
similar results.

SUBJECTS FOR PANORAMAS

When shooting 360-degree photos, it is
best to choose a subject close by, such as a
garden or courtyard enclosed by architectural
masterpieces, or a famous interior.

WEB RESOURCES

VIEW VIRTUAL REALITY PANORAMAS
To see some of the best 360-degree
photography, visit the Apple Quicktime VR
website. You'll find lots of tips on shooting
and links to panorama enthusiasts world-wide.
Go to **www.apple.com/quicktime/qtvr/**

STARTING POINT: SHOOTING

A good panorama requires plenty of advance preparation. First you
need to select a subject that maintains its interest though a 360-
degree arc, such as a cityscape, for example. Position yourself
exactly in the center of an imaginary circle, with all elements an
equal distance away from you. Use a tripod if you have one: the
camera shouldn't change position between shots.

Set your zoom lens to mid-range, rather than wide angle, and
quickly check that you can fit everything you want in the frame.
Once satisfied, leave your zoom setting unchanged throughout
shooting. You can shoot your images either in portrait (upright) or
landscape (horizontal) format, but don't change over halfway
through. Shoot your images with generous overlaps between frames.

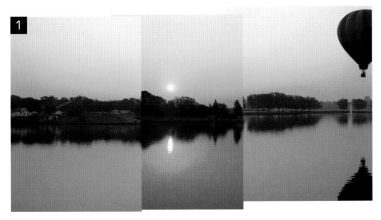

When first placed side-by-side, your source images will look very different due to the different exposures levels chosen by your camera in auto mode. Although you can adjust for these in your software, no differences will be apparent if you expose each individual slice with the exposure lock on.

1 Transfer your files to your computer and launch Spin Panorama. Open the folder of images and decide which ones should be included in the project. If you haven't shot them in sequence, you can easily alter the assembly order.

2 Next identify the Stitch Points in your overlapping images, which is a bit like aligning different strips of wallpaper. Zoom in close and identify the exact points where images should overlap or register. The Smart Stitch option will do this for you automatically, but better results are obtained if you do it manually.

3 Once you have joined the images, crop out any signs of jagged edges. Determine the Output Size, measured in pixel dimensions, and the result in one of two different formats. The Image File option allows you to save as a flat image, like a JPEG, which can be used for a printout. The VR Movie option lets you save your work as a rotating 360 VR panorama for web or on-screen use.

4 If you want to manipulate the Image File option, you can open it in any imaging application, such as Photoshop or PaintShop Pro, and add color or filter effects or remove unwanted details. To print out, you must either create a custom paper size or print out at less than 100 percent.

UNIT 13.4

CREATIVE PRINT PROJECTS →
MAKING FRAMES

WHY PRINT ALL YOUR PHOTOGRAPHS WITH STRAIGHT EDGES? TRY FRAMING THEM FIRST.

SCANNING FRAMES AND BORDERS

i | **Difficulty** > 2 or Basic–Intermediate
Time > less than 1 hour

Scanning 3D objects > go to page 34

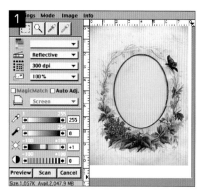

EXAMPLE 1

1 Scan a decorative mount or frame on a flatbed scanner, just as you would any other 3-D object, and scan an image or choose a photo to go in it. With software tools for retouching and repair at hand, your originals need not be in perfect condition. This mount had a ripped edge and was badly scratched. Make an RGB scan and repair any defects using your Rubber Stamp tool.

2 Make a selection of the oval aperture, then go back to the image you want to insert and **Edit>Copy**. Click into your frame image **Edit>Paste Into**. This places your image behind the oval aperture, using it like a stencil or mask, and you can move it until it sits in the right position. Once assembled, colorize and retouch any blemishes or irregularities.

USING PHOTOFRAME ONLINE

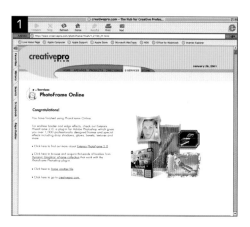

The best way to access creative software is through your web browser. You don't need to have an imaging application, just digital image files on a disk.

1 PhotoFrame is available for online use simply by visiting the CreativePro website (**www.creativepro.com**), and registering as a new user. This is free, and all you need to do is remember your log-in codes. Next click on **Services** and select **PhotoFrame Online**.

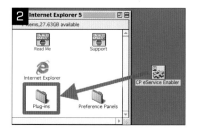

2 To use PhotoFrame you first need to download a tiny plug-in file called the CP e-Service Enabler plug-in. Click on **Download** and wait for a few minutes. Once downloaded to a Windows PC, the plug-in file, which has a tiny jigsaw icon, will be placed automatically inside the browser's plug-in folder. On a Mac, you may need to drag it there yourself, **Macintosh HD>Internet Applications>Netscape** (or Explorer, depending on which browser you are using) **>Plug-ins**.

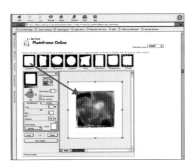

EXAMPLE 2

1 Find an empty antique photograph frame and a portrait photo in a period style, scan both, and assemble the images together.

2 Tone the portrait a copper color to mimic the look and feel of an historic photo. The portrait used here was a good choice because there is little evidence of the twenty-first century. To prevent the edges of the pasted-in image looking too sharp, feather the image inside the frame. The Layers palette shows how this project was arranged.

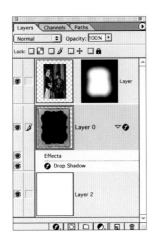

WEB RESOURCES

To download custom filters and recipes for Adobe Photoshop, visit **www.actionxchange.com**. There are thousands of items for free download to make frames, photo effects, and text effects too.

3 Quit your browser, then relaunch and go back to the CreativePro site. When prompted, simply browse for the image file you want to use, and then watch the Photoframe software load in your Browser window. You can work on images of any size. Your files are never uploaded to a remote server; they stay on your computer at all times.

4 There is a limited number of edges to choose from, but plenty of scope for creativity. Here a watercolor effect has been selected. Choose your frame, then simply drag and drop it over your image. Once you've saved the image, you can disconnect and print as normal.

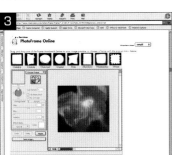

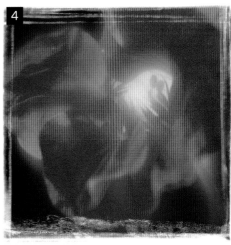

UNIT 14.1

PREPARING PHOTOS FOR EMAIL
AND THE INTERNET → SHRINKING

IF YOU WANT TO ATTACH DIGITAL PHOTOGRAPHS TO AN EMAIL OR USE THEM ON A WEB SITE, IT'S ESSENTIAL TO COMPRESS THEM FIRST.

LOSSY FILE FORMATS

JPEG is referred to as a "lossy" file format, meaning image data is lost each time the image is saved, and image quality is thereby reduced. You should always make a duplicate image file just for use on your web page or for attaching to an email, leaving the original in pristine condition.

Digital images take up a lot of data space compared to word processing documents and emails. Each time you open an image, every tiny pixel is recreated using a color recipe coded with a 24-digit number. There may be a million or more pixels in your image, so you can probably see the size of the problem.

To solve this problem digital image data can be compressed into smaller packages that take up less space, and less time to transport over a network. There are two common routines used for compressing images: JPEG and GIF. Both are available in most applications under the Save As command.

JPEG

The best compression mode to use for photographic images is the JPEG (for Joint Photographic Experts Group, named after the body that defined the standard). JPEG works by performing a calculation on a block of pixels, say 8 x 8, that results in a smaller data number describing the whole block compared to the cumulative values describing each pixel. The result is a compromise, and as such, may involve a drop in image quality. JPEGs can be saved on a scale of 0–10 or 0–100, depending on which package you use. At the bottom of the scale more space can be saved, but the image quality will be poorer. At the top, more data is saved, giving better image quality.

AN ORIGINAL UNCOMPRESSED image like this needs 6.1Mb of storage space

AFTER COMPRESSION into a JPEG, the image has been reduced to a mere 120K without too much loss of quality

CONTROLLING DATA SIZE

It's not possible to predict how much data will be created by two images with the same pixel dimensions saved in the JPEG format. If your image has multi-colored areas and fine details like a photo of a flowerbed it will create more data than a same-sized image of a blurry blue sky. Why? Because there are no sharp edges in the sky image and no colors other than blue and white. Effectively, this means data size can be further controlled by a careful choice of subject matter.

HIGHLY DETAILED IMAGES with many colors and sharp focus will compress least

BLURRED EDGED IMAGES that are constructed from fewer colors will compress more

GIF

Compression doesn't involve physically reducing the dimensions of an image, but reducing the need for a 24-digit pixel color code. Graphics Interchange Format (GIF) is usually only used for compressing solid color graphic images like logos. Unlike JPEG, it can't cope with the subtle color transitions of a color photograph.

AFTER COMPRESSION using the GIF routine the posterized colors and loss of detail are very evident

GIF compression works in a different way by limiting the color palette to 256 colors or less. Fewer colors mean less data and smaller pixel color codes. When photographs are saved as GIFs in error, you'll see the subtle range of the original's 16.7 million colors converted into 256 colors. This can make the image look patchy or patterned.

BEFORE COMPRESSION

UNIT 14.2

PREPARING PHOTOS FOR EMAIL AND THE INTERNET → SENDING IMAGES AS ATTACHMENTS

i **Difficulty** > 1 or Basic
Time > less than 30 minutes

DIGITAL IMAGE ATTACHMENTS TAKE MUCH LESS TIME TO ARRIVE AT AN OVERSEAS ADDRESS THAN A POSTCARD AND CAN ALSO BE PRINTED OUT BY THE RECIPIENT.

BEFORE RESIZING, this image measured 1800 x 1200 pixels. After reducing, the image is now physically smaller onscreen

1 Adjusting pixel dimensions
The first step is to decide how big your image will appear on your recipient's computer monitor. Some people still use a 640 x 480 VGA sized display, so in the **Image Size** dialog reduce landscape-shaped images to 600 pixels wide, and portrait-shaped images to 400 pixels high. Any bigger and the images will not fit on the receiver's screen. After resizing your digital images, it is good practice to apply the Unsharp Mask Filter to regain any sharpness lost in the process.

2 Saving as JPEGs

Next, perform a **File>Save As** command and from the File Format drop down menu, choose **JPEG**. Enter a file name, then **Save**, and wait for the Options dialog to appear. If you want the email recipient to print your image, pick a mid-range setting like 4–7, as this makes less blocky compression artefact patterns on your image. If the image is for viewing only, choose a low setting such as 0-3. Select the Standard Baseline option.

3 Checking the size indicator

Before hitting OK, check the size indicator at the bottom of the dialog. This tells you the final size of the compressed data and, most usefully, how long it's likely to take to transport via modems of differing speeds. This image was 47k and had an estimated download time of 8 seconds using a 56kbps modem.

COMPRESSING IMAGE FILES

If you are interested in learning about the latest advances in image compression technology, then visit www.luratech.com. Lurawave is a new kind of compression that dramatically chops down image data for fast network transmission or efficient storage under the JPEG 2000 banner. If you want to experiment, there are free plug-ins to download so you can customize your versions of Adobe Photoshop.

THE DIALOG BOX tells you the final size of the compressed data

4 Attaching to an email

Save your file in a clearly labeled folder on your hard drive so you know where to find it, and open your email application. Create a new message, enter the recipient's address and type your message. Finally select **Add Attachment** and browse your folders to locate your image. Select it, return to your message, connect to the Internet, and send. Outlook Express gives you a visual preview of the images chosen, but other packages might only show the file name.

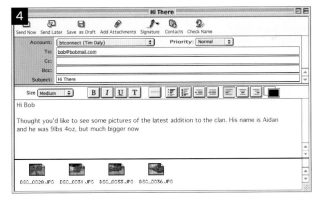

FREE EMAIL

You don't need to have special email software like Outlook Express or Eudora to send emails: you can use your web browser instead. Go to a web based email host such as Hotmail or Yahoo, and fill in the registration form. It's free, works immediately, and is accessible from any computer in the world. All you need to do is remember your user name and password each time you log on.

FREE EMAIL HOSTS

www.hotmail.com
www.yahoo.com
www.tripod.lycos.co.uk
www.freeserve.com
www.mac.com

UNIT 14.3

PREPARING PHOTOS FOR EMAIL AND THE INTERNET → WEB GALLERIES

YOU DON'T HAVE TO BE A WEB DESIGNER TO GET YOUR PHOTOGRAPHS ONTO THE INTERNET. THERE ARE LOTS OF FREELY AVAILABLE TOOLS TO DO THE HARD WORK FOR YOU.

ONLINE LABS

www.ofoto.com
www.fotowire.com
www.fotango.co.uk
www.mac.com

Web photo galleries are like online photo albums, open 24 hours to the whole world. All you need to decide is how much of the design work you want to get involved in.

ONLINE ALBUMS

Many regular photo processing labs now offer to upload your processed films freely to an Internet photo album. Others let you upload images to an Internet photo album from your computer just by using a web browser. With this type of service you don't have any control over the page design and you can't make hyperlinks to other sites, but it is the easiest way to start. Once uploaded, you can email the site URL to your friends and they can order prints direct from the online lab. There is usually a small monthly charge for this service.

CLICKING ON A THUMBNAIL brings it into the preview pane.

DIGITAL IMAGES are uploaded by modem and appear as thumbnails for review.

ONLINE GALLERIES and albums offer a great way to share your images worldwide.

TEMPLATES

If you visit a web community like Tripod or AOL, you can register for free web space and templates. Templates are preset pages that you can use to enter your own text and image content. You don't download the templates, but rather enter your own information online. Once published, your site will have its own web address (URL) which you can email to your friends. This service is usually free, but will be accompanied by advertising banners over which you've no control.

USING AUTO WEB GALLERY FUNCTIONS

If you don't want to use online templates, you can use the auto Web Gallery commands in Photoshop or other packages.

First, organize all the images you want to appear into one folder. There's no need to make your images into JPEGs first, as this will be done for you. Choose **File>Automate>Web Photo Gallery** and select the folder you've just made. You'll be offered a range of different page styles, thumbnails, and image sizes. Hit OK and watch the software do the work for you.

All site files will be created in one folder, but to upload your site you'll need to register for some free web space first, and then use a shareware FTP package to transfer your files. Paint Shop Pro users have a direct link to a free web space called www.studioavenue.com.

SERVICES TO CHOOSE FROM

www.tripod.co.uk
www.aol.com
www.geocities.com
www.freeserve.com

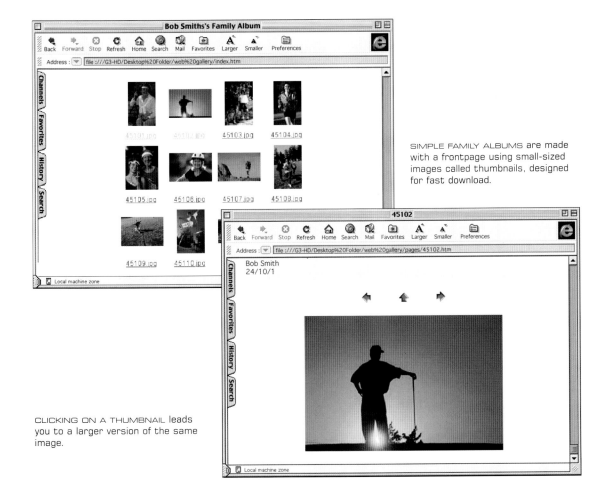

SIMPLE FAMILY ALBUMS are made with a frontpage using small-sized images called thumbnails, designed for fast download.

CLICKING ON A THUMBNAIL leads you to a larger version of the same image.

TROUBLESHOOTING →FOR COMPUTERS

YOU DON'T NEED TO BE AN EXPERT TO TROUBLESHOOT BASIC PROBLEMS
ON YOUR COMPUTER OR SYSTEM.

WEBSITES

COMPUTER HARDWARE
www.apple.com
www.ibm.com
www.toshiba.com
www.silicongraphics.com

DIGITAL CAMERAS
www.fujifilm.com
www.epson.com
www.olympus.com
www.nikon.com
www.minolta.com
www.kodak.com
www.canon.com

DIGITAL CAMERA CARD READERS
www.lexar.com

FILM SCANNERS
www.minolta.com
www.epson.com
www.nikon.com
www.canon.com

FLATBED SCANNERS
www.umax.com
www.imacon.com
www.heidelberg.com
www.epson.com
www.canon.com

IMAGING SOFTWARE
www.adobe.com
www.jasc.com
www.photosuite.com
www.extensis.com
www.corel.com

UTILITY SOFTWARE
www.norton.com
www.quicktime.com

Q. When using image manipulation software, my computer slows down and seems to take forever to perform a command. What causes this to happen?
A. There are several possible reasons, but the most likely is a shortage of memory. Close all other applications to free up system memory and make sure you are working on files on your hard drive, rather than on removable media. Check your hard drive for free space: if you find less than 100Mb, erase unwanted files to free up space. Finally, check the amount of RAM installed on your machine. Less then 64Mb is impractical for working with image files and you should buy additional memory.

Q. My computer is slow to start up and works lethargically in all applications.
A. Your hard disk could be fragmented, with many small portions of data written in non-contiguous sectors. Defragment the disk using a maintenance routine such as Norton Utilities. You should see an immediate improvement.

Q. Since I bought a new scanner my computer keeps crashing.
A. This sounds like a conflict between different driver software. Search the scanner manufacturer's website for an update or "patch." These are usually downloadable free of charge.

Q. Why do some fonts look jagged on my monitor?
A. This happens if you don't use a package like Adobe Type Manager (ATM), which smooths all onscreen fonts for easier use. ATM Light is often bundled freely with Adobe applications.

Q. Why can't my Windows computer read Mac disks and media?
A. Windows PCs can't read Mac disks, but Macs can read PC-formatted media. If you need to swap disks between the two platforms, always use PC-formatted disks and put file extensions on the end of your documents.

Q. My hard disk is full but I don't know which files to throw away.
A. When a computer crashes it creates huge files—called temporary files or .tmps—in an attempt to rescue lost data. If left untended these can quickly fill up your drive. Search for files and folders over a certain size, say 10Mb, or with the extension ".tmp". Delete these to free up space.

Q. I've thrown some important files away by mistake. Is there any way of getting them back again?
A. Probably. Provided you haven't used your computer much since your mistake, the data should still be there on your disk, albeit invisible. Use the UnErase application in Norton Utilities to retrieve the lost data to a different disk. If you saved other files or installed new software in the intervening time, the new data may have written over your lost files.

GLOSSARY

BIT A binary digit, the smallest unit of digital data, capable of expressing one of two states, like on or off, or if used to describe color, black or white.

BITMAP All digital images are made from pixels arranged in a chessboard-like grid called a bitmap.

BITMAP MODE The bitmap image mode can capture only two colors—black and white—and is the only one you should use to scan line art.

BURST RATE An indication of the speed at which a camera can save image data then get ready to capture the next shot (see Recovery Time).

BYTE A binary term, eight bits of digital data, expressing 2^8, or 256 different states or colors.

CCD A Charge-Coupled Device is the light-sensitive receptor in a digital camera or scanner.

CD-R Compact Disk Recordable is the cheapest and most cost-effective type of media for storing digital images. You need to have a CD writer to write data to these disks, but they can all be played back in a standard CD-ROM drive.

CD-RW Compact Disk ReWritable is a more versatile media than CD-R. CD-RWs can be written to, erased, then filled up again, much like a floppy disk. They have the same 640Mb capacity as CD-Rs.

CIS Contact Image Sensors, recently introduced alternatives to CCDs, are used in scanner technology and give high resolution values.

CMYK MODE Cyan, Magenta, Yellow, and Black (called K to prevent confusion with Blue) is an image mode used in preparation for lithographic reproduction. Most books and magazines are printed using the litho process and CMYK inks.

COMPACTFLASH The thicker type of removable memory card used in many digital cameras (see SmartMedia).

COMPRESSION Large digital files are routinely compressed using a mathematical algorithm to reduce their data size. This enables you (for example) to squeeze more images onto your removable media.

DPI (SCANNER) The maximum resolution of a film or flatbed scanner is measured in dots per inch. The higher the number, the more data you can extract from the original, and the larger your prints can be without loss of quality.

DPI (PRINTER) DPI also describes the maximum number of separate droplets an inkjet printer can spray onto a given media.

DPI (IMAGE FILE) The pixels in a digital image can be made smaller or larger by altering their spatial resolution. Sometimes referred to as pixels per inch or ppi.

DPOF Digital Print Order Format is a recently devised set of universal standards allowing you to specify print options directly from your camera.

EXPOSURE Correct exposure is defined as the exact quantity of light required to make a good picture. It is achieved by selecting the right combination of shutter speed and aperture value.

FILE FORMAT Digital images can be created and saved in many different file formats such as JPEG, TIFF, PSD, etc. Formats are designed to let you package images for their future purpose, such as email, print, or web viewing.

FIREWIRE Also known as IEEE 1394, this is a fast computer interface for transferring large amounts of data. FireWire ports are usually found only on high-end digital cameras and video cameras.

FLASHPATH An adaptor made from a 3.5 in floppy disk drive modified to accept SmartMedia memory cards and used for transferring digital data to your PC through its floppy disk drive. Works at snail's pace.

FLASHPIX A file format invented by Kodak/HP to create digital camera files. These files can only be opened in a compatible application.

GIF Graphics Interchange Format is a small, low-resolution file type used to save graphics and logos for web pages.

GIGABYTE A gigabyte (Gb) is 1024 megabytes.

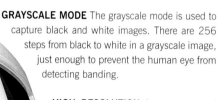

GRAYSCALE MODE The grayscale mode is used to capture black and white images. There are 256 steps from black to white in a grayscale image, just enough to prevent the human eye from detecting banding.

HIGH RESOLUTION Images captured at high resolution give the highest quality reproduction in print. Their disadvantage is their sheer size— each may contain a million or more pixels, and this puts enormous strain on disk capacity.

HOTSHOE A universal socket for attaching an external flashgun to better digital cameras.

IBM MICRODRIVE A "mini hard drive," or removable media, used in digital cameras, available in capacities of up to 1Gb.

INTERPOLATION All digital images can be enlarged, or interpolated, by introducing new "invented" pixels to the bitmap grid. Interpolated images never have the same sharp qualities or color accuracy of original non-interpolated images.

JPEG A universal format for compressed image files, defined by the Joint Photographic Experts Group (hence the acronym). Most digital cameras save images as JPEG files to make more efficient use of limited-capacity memory cards.

JUMPSHOT CABLE A low-cost, high-performance USB digital card reader made by Lexar.

LINE ART Artwork created with only one color and no continuous tone.

LITHIUM A type of rechargeable battery used in digital cameras.

LOW RESOLUTION Low-resolution images have the advantage of small file size, but their lower quality makes them suitable only for web viewing.

MEGABYTE A megabyte (Mb) is 1024 kilobytes.

MEGAPIXEL One million pixels, used to describe the sensitivity of the CCD in a digital camera. A camera capable of producing a non-interpolated image of 2,048 x 1,536 pixels is described as a 3.14 (usually rounded up to 3.2) Megapixel camera.

MEMORY STICK A proprietory type of removable media made by Sony for use in their digital cameras and digital video cameras.

NICAD High energy rechargeable batteries commonly used in digital cameras and laptop computers, made from **ni**ckel-**cad**mium cells.

OPTICAL RESOLUTION Sometimes called true resolution, this refers to the non-interpolated pixel dimensions of an image.

PARALLAX Parallax error occurs in cameras fitted with optical viewfinders set above, or to one side of, the lens. When used in close focus, what you see through the viewfinder is different to the image captured by the lens, which accounts for the chopped-off heads and other mutilations sometimes seen in amateur photographs.

PARALLEL A largely outdated interface mainly associated with older printers and scanners. Parallel connections give the slowest rate of data transfer.

PCI SLOT The Peripheral Component Interface slots found in better computers allow you to add to and upgrade your system.

PCMCIA Also known as a PC card, this is a high capacity removable media designed for use in professional digital cameras. Unlike solid-state SmartMedia and CompactFlash cards, PC cards have moving internal parts like mini hard disks. Most good quality laptops have a PCMCIA port for reading cards directly.

PIXEL From **Pic**ture **El**ement, the pixel is the smallest component of a digital image. Pixel color is determined by a "recipe" using three ingredients: red, green, and blue.

PIXELLATION When a digital print is made from a low-res image, fine details appear blocky or pixellated because not enough pixels were used to describe complex shapes.

PLUG-IN A piece of software that adds extra functions to your favorite application.

RAM Random Access Memory, sometimes described as "working memory," is where your computer holds data immediately before and after processing, and before the computation is "written" (or saved) to disk. The more RAM you have, the more applications you can run, and the easier it is to open and manipulate large files.

RECOVERY TIME The minimum time your camera requires between shots to save captured image data to memory.

REMOVABLE MEMORY CARDS Digital cameras have removable memory cards sold in varying capacities, from 8Mb to 32Mb and above. Bigger cards are more expensive, but allow you to shoot more images before transferring to a computer or other storage device.

RESOLUTION The term used to describe image quality, which itself is determined by pixel quantity.

RGB MODE Red, Green, Blue is the standard mode for capturing and processing color images. Each separate color has its own 256-step range.

SCSI Small Computer Systems Interface is a now nearly obsolete interface used for attaching scanners and other peripherals to your computer. It has been displaced by USB and FireWire.

SERIAL Another obsolete interface, or connector, used for attaching printers and other peripherals to your computer. Serial data transfer is much slower than SCSI and USB.

SMARTMEDIA The thinner type of removable memory cards, available in various sizes up to 128Mb (*see* CompactFlash).

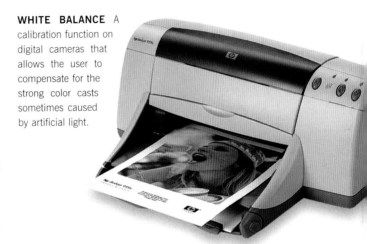

TIFF The Tagged Image File Format is a universal standard file format used in desktop publishing.

TWAIN The interestingly-named Toolkit Without an Interesting Name is the software equivalent of a travel plug adapter, allowing TWAIN-compliant devices like scanners and digital cameras to communicate with applications like Photoshop.

USB Slower than FireWire, but hugely faster than SCSI, parallel, and serial interfaces, the universal serial bus allows "plug-and-play" connection of peripherals. Older systems like SCSI could only be plugged in when the computer was switched off.

WHITE BALANCE A calibration function on digital cameras that allows the user to compensate for the strong color casts sometimes caused by artificial light.

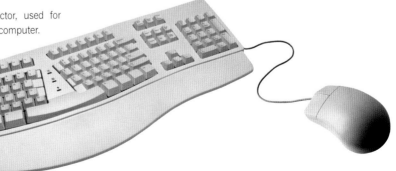

INDEX

Figures in italics indicate captions; those in bold type indicate main references.

3-D objects, scanning 34-5
3-D rendering 94-5

A
acetates 117
add-ons 11, 14–15
adding interest *59, 59*
Adobe Gamma color calibration application 13
Adobe PhotoDeluxe 38
Adobe Photoshop **46–7**
Adobe Photoshop Elements **44–5**
Adobe Type Manager (ATM) 136
Advanced Photo System (APS) format 36, 37
Airbrush tool 72, 91, 94
albums, online 134, *134*, 135
Andromeda 41
AOL 135
aperture 54, *55, 57*
Apple iMac *12*
Apple Mac **16**, *16*, **17**, 37, 136
Art History brush 91
artists' papers 117, 119, *119*, **124–5**
artwork, scanning 33
asymmetry *59, 59*
Auto Contrast *31*
auto-adjust controls (scanner) 31
autofocus errors 62, *62*

B
backgrounds, adding interest 108–9
banner printing 115
batteries, rechargeable 19, 20, 21
battery charger *19*, 20, 21
bird's-eye view *58*
Bitmap mode 31, *31*
blending modes 73
Blur tool 91
booklets 125
books, scanning color prints 33
brightness sliders 31
brushes 72, 76–7
bundles 10

C
cable converter *37*
calibration tools 13
Canon 14, 21
    papers 116, *116*, 117
canvas cloth inkjet media *117*
captions 123, *123*
capture modes 31
capture resolution 30, 31
card reader **15**, *15, 19*, **27**, *27*
cards 125
cathode ray tube (CRT) 12, 13
CD writers 15
CD-R disks 15, *15*, 17
CD-ROM drive and disk *15*
cell phone network 21
Channel Mixer 104, *104*
charged couple device (CCD) 19, 28
clipboard 39, 80
cloning 39
Cloud filter 105, *105*
CMYK color set 89, 114, 115, 118
color
    computer monitors 13
    improving photographs 69, *69*
    palette 72, *72*
    portrait coloring effects 100–101
    scanners' color depth 29
Color Balance adjustment 74–5, 119
coloring photographs
    global color change and sepia 74–5
    hand coloring with brushes 76–7
    multiple coloring with commands and selections 78–9
    tools 72–3
ColorMailer Photo Service software 121
compact-type camera **20**, *20*, 22, 23
CompactFlash cards *19*, 20, 26
composition 66
compression of images 121, 133
computer transfer 20, 21
computers
    computer platforms 16–17
    external add-ons 14–15
    internal components 10–11
    memory 136
    monitors, color, and keyboard 12–13
    purchasing tips 10
    troubleshooting 136
contrast adjustment 68, *68*
contrast sliders 31
contrast tools 65, *65*
copy and paste 39, *39*, 80, 84, 85
Corel KPT 6.0 41
CorelDraw 41
creative effects
    3-D rendering and warping 94–5
    filters 88–9
    making a watercolor painting 90–91
    psychedelic color, sharpness, and brightness 92–3
creative print projects
    making frames 128–9
    panoramas 126–7
    tools 122–3
    using art papers 124–5
crop tool 64, 66
cropping *64*, 66, *66, 67*
crossover technology 21
cutting and masking 38

D
dark prints 107
data size, controlling 131, *131*
day into night, transforming 106–7
deckled edges 125
defocusing 103
defragmentation 136
depth of field 55, *55*
Difference layer blending mode 93
diffused focus 103
digital cameras
    camera functions 22–3
    care of 53
    holding your camera 52
    image capture quality 24–5
    purchasing tips 20
    transferring photos to your computer 26–7

types of cameras 20–21
    what is a digital camera? 18–19
digital wallet 27
digital zooms 24, *24*
distortion 57, *57*
docking station 20
downloading 27, *27*
dpi (dots per inch) 28, *28*, 29, *29*, 118, 119
driver software, installing 27
driver updates 26, 37
dynamic range 12

E
editing 23
email attachments 14, 19, 24
    compressing digital photographs 130–31
    free email 133
    sending 132–3
enlargement, scanner 31
Epson 14
    papers 116, *116*, 117
Epson Stylus Photo printer 115
Eraser tool 38, 77, 85, 109, 110
Eudora 133
expansion bay 11
exposure problems 63, *63*
Extensis Photoframe 2.0 40, 45, 91
Eyedropper tool 72, *72*, 94

F
Fabriano artists' watercolor paper 117
feathering 72, 80
file extensions 17
file size 31, *31*
Fill command 73
filters 39, *39*
    Anti-Alias 68
    artist 88, *88*
    brushstroke 89, *89*
    Cloud 105, *105*
    distortion 88, *88*
    filter fading 89, *89*
    filtering type 89, *89*
    flash 61
    Motion Blur 105, *105*
    pixel 88, *88*
    sharpening 65, *65*
    texture 88, *88*

"warm-up" 74
Firewire connection 11, 15, 21, 28, 37
flash 20, 22, 24, 25, **60–61**
flashgun 21, 22
flashpath adapter 15
floppy disks 15, *15*, 17
focal length 56, *56*
focus 20, 21, **56–7**, *57*
    defocusing 103
    diffused 103
frames, making 128–9
Fuji 21
Fuji Frontier digital mini-lab 120

G
GIF (Graphics Interchange Format) 43, 45, 131, *131*
glossary 137–9
Gradient tool 73, 79
Grayscale mode 31, *31*, 74, 75, 76

H
hard disk/drive 11, *11*
Heidelberg 14
History palette 71
Hotmail 133
Hue blending mode 93

I
IBM Microdrive 21
Ilford papers 117
image capture quality 24–5
Image Correction and Enhancement (ICE) 37
improving photographs
    color and contrast 68–9
    cropping and resizing 66–7
    sharpening up 70–71
    tools 64–5
Inkjetmall website 116
input resolution 30
Interactive Warp 94
Internet
    attachments 24
    connection 14
    see also email attachments
Internet Explorer 121
interpolation 29, *29*

ISO (International Standards Organisation) speeds 22, *22*, 24, 71, *71*

J
JPEG format 37, 71, *71*, 121, 130, *130*, 131, 133, 135

K
keyboard 13, *13*
Kodak
    papers 117
    photo labs 121
Kodak Photo CD 37, 71
Kodak Picture CD 37

L
La Ciè 13
landscapes and places
    adding interest to backgrounds 108–9
    reflections and water 110–11
    tools 104–5
    turning day into night 106–7
Lasso tool 38, 96, 108, 109
layers 38, 77, 80–81, *80*, *81*
    adjustment 78
    invert adjustment layer 92
    Layer blends 83
    Layer Effects 83
    multiple layered landscape 86–7
LCD (liquid crystal display) **19**, 20
lens flare 53, *53*
lenses 20, *20*, 21, *21*, 24
    changing 57
    clean 53, *53*
    dirty 53, *53*
    "fish-eye" 57
    macro *56*
    obstructions 25
    telephoto 56, 57
    wide-angle *56*, 57
    zoom 56, 57
lighting 21, 22, 23, *23*, 25, **52–3**
lines 58, *58*
Linux 11
lithographs 117
Luminosity blend 85, 93
Lyson inkjet art media 117

M

Mac OS 11
magazines, scanning color prints 33
Magic Wand tool 38, *38*, *105*, 106, 109
Magnetic Lasso 106
marquee tool 30, 35, 38, *38*, 94, 96
masks 92, 93
memory cards 15, 19, 20, 21, 23, **26**, *26*, 27, *27*, 115, *115*
Memory Stick 20
MGI PhotoSuite **42–3**
Microsoft Windows 11, 16, 17
    see also Windows PCs
Mitsubishi 13
mixing, merging, and montage
    multiple layered landscape 86–7
    text effects 82–3
    textured and translucent overlays 84–5
    tools 80–81
mobile phone 19
modems, internal 14
monitors 12–13, *13*
Motion Blur filter 105, *105*
mouse 13, *13*
movies, making 19
MP3 music files 21
MPEG format 23

N

negatives 36
Netscape Communicator 121
Nikon D1 camera 21
"noise" 71, *71*
Norton Utilities 136

O

OCR (Optical Character Recognition) software 31
opacity 73, *73*, 81, 83, 85, 93
operating systems 11
optical value *29*, 29
Outlook Express 133
overexposure 63
overlays, textured and translucent 84–5

P

Paintbrush tool 72
Paintbucket/Flood tool 73
Painter 41
painting 39
PaintShop Pro 41, **48–9**, 77, 135
panoramas 126–7
panoramic stitching 43, 56
paper sizes 116, 125
papers 116–17, 124–5
Parallel port 11, 15, 28
PCI expansion slot 37
PCs (personal computers) 16, 17
Pen tool 87
Pencil tool 72
people and portraits
    coloring effects 100–101
    selections 96–7
    tone effects 98–9
    vignettes and diffused focus 102–3
peripheral cabling *10*
peripherals 11, 14–15
photo labs, online 120–21
photo problems 62–3
Photo-Paint 41
PhotoFrame Online 91
photographs
    scanning 32–3
    see also coloring photographs; improving photographs
pixels **19**, 20, 21, 28, 29, 31, 36
    altering dimensions *67*, *67*, 132, *132*
    filters 88, *88*
    and vectors 83
plug-ins 14
portraits *see* people and portraits
ports 11, *11*, 28
power adaptor 19, *19*, 20
preview
    digital camera 19, 20, 22, *22*
    print 122, *122*
printers 10, 11
    card reader 115, *115*
    card-slot 15
    inkjet **15**, *15*, 75, **114–15**, *114*, *115*
    mini 25
printing out
    frequently asked questions 118–19
    how printers work 114–15
    print media 116–17
    using online photo labs 120–21
processor 10
program modes 54

Q

QuickTime *23*
QuickTime Virtual Reality Studio 126

R

RAM (Random Access Memory) 10, *10*, 136
red eye 62, *62*
reflections 111
resampling 67
reshooting 25
resizing 67, *67*
resolution
    camera 20, 21
    and printing out 118–19, *119*
    scanner 28–9, *28*, *29*, 30
Retouch tool 72, 73
RGB mode 31, *31*, 74, 75, 76, 89, 118
Rives artists' watercolor paper 117
roll paper adaptor 115, *115*
Rotate command 86
Rubber Stamp tool **65**, *65*, 76, 106, 110, 128

S

saturation values 75
scanners 10, 11
    combination 28
    conflict with computer 136
    film **14**, *14*, 28, 36-7
    flatbed **14**, *14*, **28–9**, *29*
scanning
    3-D objects 34–5
    film 36–7
    flatbed 28–9
    photographs and artwork 32–3
    scan-to-disk services 37
    scanner controls 30–31
    software 37
screen resolution 13
screenprinting 117
SCSI connector 11, 28, 37
selecting part of image 38, *38*
selective focus 57, *57*
Serial port 11, 15

CREDITS

Quarto would like to thank and acknowledge the following for the pictures reproduced in this book:

Key; t=top, c=center, b=bottom, l=left, r=right

Apple Computers: 8 bc, 12l, 16, 138 c;
Belkin: 10 cl, bl, 138 bl;
Canon: 1, 14 l, 25 b, 116, 139 tr;
Compaq: 11 tr, 13 tr, 17;
Epson: 4 b, 114 bl, br, 115, 117 t, bc, b;
Fuji: 4 t, 8 tc, 15 tl, 18, 19 tr, cr, br, 20 tr, 21 tr;
Imation: 15 bl;
Iomega International sa: 15 cr, br, bc, 27 b, 137 t;
Kodak: 3, 20 bc, 22 bl, 37 b, 50 b;
Lexar Media: 8 t, 19 bc, 26, 27 t, 115 br, 137 b, 138 t;
Minolta (UK) Ltd: 21 l;
PC World: 11 tl,bl, 15 tr (Hewlett Packard), 29 b, 37 t, 139 c (Hewlett Packard);
Umax: 14 r;

Whilst every effort has been made to credit the pictures, we apologize in advance if there have been any omissions or errors

Shadow Intensity slider 90
shareware 14
shareware FTP packages 135
sharing images 121
sharpening filters 25, *25*
sharpening up photographs 70–71
shooting around your subject 59
shutter, electronic 22
shutter speed 24, **54–5**, *54*, *55*
single lens reflex (SLR) type camera
    21, *21*, 22
sketchpad papers 125
slides 36, *36*
SmartMedia cards *19*, 20, 26, *26*
Smudge tool 90
software applications
    Adobe Photoshop **46–7**
    Adobe Photoshop Elements **44–5**
    MGI PhotoSuite **42–3**
    PaintShop Pro 7 41, **48–9**
    preview and plug-in applications
        40–41
    universal commands and tools
        38–9
software updates 14
Somerset inkjet art media 117
Sony 13, 20
sound clips 23
Spin Panorama 126, 127
Sponge tool 72, *72*, 91, 107
storing images 19, 121
swapping files between two platforms 17
swatches 77
symmetry 59, *59*, 66

T
templates, Internet 135
temporary files 136
test print 124, *124*
thin film transistor (TFT) 12
3-D objects, scanning 34–5
TIFF file format 27
Tint Touchup brush 77
tone effects 98–9
transfer time 121
Tripod 135
TWAIN 30
Type layers 82, 83, 89
Type Mask tool 83

U
Umax 14
underexposure 63
UnErase application 136
Unix 11
Unsharp Mask Filter (USM) 37,
    70–71, *70*
URL 134, 135
USB port 11, 15, 28

V
vectors 82, 83, 89
video clips 23, *23*
Video Out 19, 22, 23
video-editing software 16
viewpoint 58, *58*
vignettes 102

W
water 110–11
"watercolor painting" 90–91
web addresses 136
Web galleries 134-5, *134*
web sites, creating 14
white balance 23, 24
Windows Media Player *23*
Windows PCs **16**, **17**, *17*, 37, 136
    see also Microsoft Windows
worm's-eye view *58*
writing papers 125

X
Xenofex 41

Y
Yahoo 133

Z
Zip disks 15, *15*, 17
Zip drive 15, *15*
zoom 24, *24*
Zoom tool 77